THE STRANGEST OF PLACES

BUILDING CASTLES MADE OF
SAND IN AFGHANISTAN

COLONEL GERALD N. CAROZZA, JR.
UNITED STATES ARMY (RETIRED)

The Strangest of Places – Building Castles Made of Sand in Afghanistan
By Colonel Gerald (Jerry) N. Carozza, Jr.
United States Army Reserve (Retired)

The views expressed herein do not reflect the views of the United States Government, the Department of Defense or the United States Army.

ISBN 978-1-66780-210-7
eBook ISBN 978-1-66780-211-4

Jerry Carozza is a retired Colonel from the U.S. Army Reserve's Judge Advocate General Corps, "the Army's law firm." He was also qualified as a Civil Affairs officer at the John F. Kennedy Special Warfare School and Center. Jerry held a wide variety of legal and non-legal assignments during his 26-year career. His most recent assignment was as the senior legal advisor to the Afghan National Army as part of the NATO Training Mission in Afghanistan. Jerry also manages fidelity and surety bond claims for a major carrier. He is a member of the New Jersey and Pennsylvania Bars. Jerry earned a Bachelor of Arts from Boston University and a Juris Doctorate from Villanova University. His military awards include the Legion of Merit, the Defense Meritorious Service Medal, the Joint Service Commendation Medal, the Afghan Campaign Medal and the NATO Non-Article 5 Medal.

Special thanks to Ed Cafasso, Matthew Glotfelter and Kery Sapet for their help in editing this work.

INTRODUCTION

August 21, 2021

I finished this book in 2012 and, except for this intro, I have not added to it or modified its narrative. The United States' castles made of sand in Afghanistan have this month vanished quicker than even I expected. As I write these words, I am bombarded with messages from Afghanistan as people I know and members of their families are desperately trying to get to the airport in Kabul in the hopes of getting a flight out of Afghanistan.

I came home from Afghanistan in 2011 and started writing this book as therapy. When I finished in 2012, I wanted to get it out there to shed light on this tragic effort doomed to failure on the course taken by our national institutions. One author who I admire, Bing West, read my manuscript in 2012 and commented that unless you were the guy who killed Bin Laden, it will be a tough sell to publishers because people were tired of Iraq and Afghanistan – no one cared anymore. That was in part the theme of my writing, that if people cared and paid real attention to our folly, they would put a stop to it. Bing's words proved true as I got that very feedback from publishing houses. As Afghanistan came to the forefront of public attention, I decided to blow the dust off this piece and again try to get the word out in the hopes of fostering some real lessons learned.

A series of reports in the Washington Post from December 2019 that reference "secret" documents showing the leadership of the U.S. Military knew all along that the effort to build Afghan security forces was failing have received new attention. What is sad is that Congress knew also. The hearings on July 24, 2012 and September 12, 2012 before the House Committee on Oversight and Government Reform on the "Dawood National Military Hospital Afghanistan: What Went Wrong?" brought the military's dishonesty to Congress' doorstep.

Prior to my testifying on July 24, 2012, I met with the chief of staff of a Republican congressman from Florida with whom I had a personal connection. I shared with him the details of my experience, much of which you are about to read. He shook his head and said that it was consistent with the many reports they have received from people returning from Afghanistan. He told me both side of the aisle, Democrat and Republicans know about the folly, but neither side was willing to stop it for fear of how the other side would take political advantage by declaring them weak and unpatriotic. I found it pathetic and cowardly. A plague on both their houses, indeed both of OUR houses.

At the conclusion of the July 24, 2012 hearing, my fellow officers that testified felt encouraged from the feedback we got from the members of the committee. We thought, maybe, finally, the American people will wake up and our futile efforts in Afghanistan will either get better focused or stop. Unfortunately, the day before the follow-up hearing on the Afghan scandal, militants killed the U.S. Ambassador to Libya and three others in Benghazi.

At the hearing on September 12, 2012, Democrats on the committee threw softball questions to the generals, eager to put behind what they perceived to be anti-Obama attacks by Republicans. The sub-committee chair Jason Chaffetz appeared tired and off his game, perhaps having spent the night monitoring events in Benghazi. He fumbled his questioning, getting dates wrong allowing the generals to cut short the line of questions. After that hearing, the focus of the Committee and the House immediately shifted to Benghazi, and there it stayed for four years to find out why four people died at a CIA run mission to supply arms to rebels in Syria. While members of Congress played politics with their investigatory powers, our efforts in Afghanistan continued at the 10 billion dollar a month clip, with over 250 U.S. military killed in action since 2012. That does not include civilians, wounded, suicides and other costs to our heroes in uniform.

Now comes the blame game: some want to blame Biden for a pull out that did not foresee the quick collapse of the Afghan government; others want to blame Trump for his deal with the Taliban devil; many want to blame the military for their less than candid reporting on their "progress;" and there is Pakistan. As Hemmingway challenged Americans to ponder for whom the bell tolls, I do the same. Ask not for whom the blame belongs, it belongs to thee. Disengagement from military actions taken overseas enabled this catastrophic failure. Uttering the phrase "thank you for your service" while nice, is not enough engagement to make a difference.

What will be the lessons learned? I hope one is in the military where they can teach that courage is not just a willingness to die in battle, but a willingness to be truthful even if it means not getting promoted or losing your job. Americans need to stop rewarding political careerism that rewards partisan cowardice like I witnessed in 2012 and we have all seen much of it since on both sides of the aisle. And, in my not so humble opinion, we need to bring back the draft. Americans need to have skin in the game, even if it is a low probability. A draft is expensive. It creates higher training and administrative costs for the military dealing with folks who would rather be elsewhere. However, the cost of not having the American people more vested in the conduct of foreign affairs is at least two trillion dollars, thousands of lives lost or damaged forever and damage to U.S. prestige. What is the price tag for that?

CONTENTS

PROLOGUE

"But I don't want to go among mad people,"
Alice remarked.
"Oh, you can't help that," said the Cat:
"we're all mad here. I'm mad. You're mad."
"How do you know I'm mad?" said Alice.
"You must be," said the Cat,
"or you wouldn't have come here."
Alice's Adventures in Wonderland

I sat at my computer, still feeling the adrenalin rush that had over-whelmed me and my interpreter, Popal, just moments before.

A young Afghan man who seemed out of place in so many ways had suddenly approached us in the Ministry of Defense compound. Carrying a bag, dressed in old worn western garb and without the customary greet-ings that roll off the tongue of an Afghan greeting another Afghan, he suddenly turned 180 degrees towards us. He began asking Popal about the differences between officers and sergeants, and between sergeants and enlisted soldiers.

I wanted to draw my weapon on him as I checked his bag for wires and scanned his chest for hidden explosives. I looked from the corner of my eye at the Afghan soldiers at the gate who just let this man into the "secure" area. Ever aware of the recent tensions from Afghan soldiers and police who had turned their weapons on Americans, Brits, Germans and Spaniards, I chose instead to backpedal steadily from the young man, rather than risk drawing fire from the Afghan soldiers who might mistake my actions as an American threatening an "innocent" civilian or who might simply welcome the excuse to shoot an American.

I thought to myself, "Really God? Is this how it ends, just days before I go home?"

As we moved closer to the gate, the man suddenly, and briskly, walked away from us and toward the ministry buildings. A rant burst from Popal: "People think because I live and work in Kabul that I am safe! But you see I am not safe! That guy, nobody checked that guy! They let anybody in. They don't check him!"

Later that morning, the intel cell issued a warning about two suicide bombers in Western dress believed to be targeting a U.S. or Afghan facility in the Green Zone. After reporting my encounter to the staff, I closed my eyes and thought of home. The visions were intense, as if I were in my driveway looking at the ferns and rock formations on either side. I had to open my eyes quickly to remind myself I wasn't there yet, and to remain vigilant until, God willing, I left this strange land — a land where a healthcare provider might punch a patient in the face for complaining that he can't afford the bribe demanded for treatment, or where a young dancing boy who performs sexual favors is a symbol of power and prestige.

Eight six weeks later I was home, receiving news of a suicide bomber who went into the Ministry of Defense headquarters and attempted to kill an Afghan with whom I had worked closely. Reflecting on the long strange trip that was my tour of duty, I decided to make good on a promise to my colleagues to tell a story that needed to be told.

Popal doing simultaneous translation at the InterContinental Hotel in Kabul, Afghanistan

CHAPTER 1

THE LAND IN BETWEEN

"Clowns to the left of me, jokers to the right,
here I am, stuck in the middle with you."

Gerry Rafferty

The good soldier must prepare his mind for the new world he is about to enter and influence - and to consider how that world will influence him. For deployments, the Army provides computer-based training and suggested readings on culture and language to shed light on the people and history of the country involved.

There is no shortage of material on Afghanistan, much of it written in the decade since the U.S. first engaged there in September 2001. But some of the most invaluable insights on what I call "the land in between" were written over a hundred years earlier by Winston Churchill, who, as a war correspondent, accompanied the British Army into Afghanistan. This chapter is not an academic treatise on Afghan history, but a ground-level assessment of a land that has frustrated the world's great armies over the course of history, a land and a culture that has embroiled the United States in its longest war. Call it "Afghanistan for Dummies."

Afghanistan is a land where tribe and village are of paramount importance, at least with today's adult Afghan population. There are four major ethnic groups or "tribes" as referred to by the Afghans: Pashtuns, Tajiks, Hazaras, and Uzbeks. The Pashtuns are the largest group, making up an estimated 43% of the population, although if you ask Pashtuns, they will likely insist the number approaches 60%. The Tajiks represent an estimated 28% of the population, the Hazaras 15% and the Uzbeks 8%. A more revealing statistic is that 72% of all Afghans cannot read. Compare that to Libya or Iraq where illiteracy affects only 20% of the population.

The Taliban, which loosely means "students of the Koran," are almost all Pashtun, although not all Pashtuns are Taliban. The Pashtuns' primary language is Pashto and they historically have ruled what is today known as Afghanistan. President Hamed Karzai (2002 to 2014) is Pashtun on his father's side and therefore considered Pashtun — although not Pashtun enough for many Taliban Pashtuns. After 9-11, the U.S. elevated Karzai, a western-educated man who can speak English, French, Urdu, Pashto and Dari, to the interim presidency in the hopes that he could persuade most of the Pashtuns to support a moderate, non-Taliban government.

The Pashtuns outside of Kabul live by a warrior code called Pashtunwali that has been woven into their version of Islam. A rugged cavernous area of land known as Pashtunistan covers parts of eastern Afghanistan and western Pakistan, where Pashtuns traverse with no sense of international border. Today, Pashtuns live in large numbers throughout Afghanistan. Centuries ago, the King of Afghanistan had Pashtuns settle all regions in an effort to strengthen Pashtun dominance. There is an overwhelming Pashtun population in the southern provinces of Afghanistan, including Helmand and Kandahar. Much of the U.S. and coalition firepower has been focused on the Taliban strongholds in the provinces of Helmand and Kandahar.

Tajiks are indigenous to the northern parts of Afghanistan, concentrated in the Panjshir valley. They speak Dari, the language of poets and the language of most professionals and educated people in Afghanistan. Dari is an ambiguous language by western standards. It has a limited number of words and tends to the passive voice, more so than Pashto. The lead ethnic group of the Northern Alliance, the Tajiks, were fiercely anti-Taliban prior to 9-11 and remain so today. Some might say Tajiks are anti-Pashtun. Hazaras are believed to be descendants of Genghis Khan and his invading army. They are mostly Shia Muslim and have an affinity for their fellow Shia brothers in Iran. If you read "The Kite Runner," the servants of the main character were Hazara. The Uzbeks, also of the north, round out the Northern Alliance and find some degree of political alliance in Turkmenistan and Turkey.

In the last 150 years, Afghanistan has been and remains a place cursed by its landlocked and mountainous geography, history and a toxic mix of illiteracy and Islam. It can hardly be called a country in the academic sense of a nation-state. One of the key elements of sovereignty is the ability to control territory - something the Government of the Islamic Republic of Afghanistan cannot do for itself. Outside of Kabul, residents residing in Afghanistan refer to President Karzai as the "Mayor of Kabul."

In a speech on the first anniversary of the formation of the NATO Training Mission in Afghanistan, then Afghan Minister of Defense Rahim Wardak boasted of the "unconquerable Afghanistan." It is unconquerable because it is cursed. It is cursed because it is unconquerable. Landlocked and infested with land pirates, Afghanistan has nothing the world wants enough to overcome the high cost of extraction and transport - with the exception of opium. There is simply nothing worth conquering. The cost of conquest was always too high and the return simply too low, thus perpetuating a chronic lack of progress. Yet, on a semi-regular basis over the course of history, nations have tried to control or influence it. There are reasons, of course, but they always involve what lies outside of Afghanistan's borders rather than the land itself.

Centuries ago, Afghanistan was a kingdom that encompassed parts of Iran, half of India, including all of what is now Pakistan, and extended north into what is now Uzbekistan and Tajikistan. King Ahmad Shah Durrani ruled this greater Afghanistan from Kandahar, the province which later would be home to Mullah Omar and his Taliban. King Ahmad Shah Durrani had scores of wives and many sons. When he died, succession was far from orderly, resulting in chaos and blood feuds between the brothers and their clans that would haunt what was left of Afghanistan ever since.

The British Empire of the 1700s through the early 1900s took an interest in Afghanistan to protect their precious jewel colony of India, which included what is now Pakistan. The British, feeling threatened by King Ahmad Shah's expansion to the edges of the East India Company's franchise, fostered the fracturing distrust among the king's sons after his death. The British used guns, commerce and diplomacy to disable Afghanistan as a threat and make it a reliable buffer between Russia and the British colony of India.

As they did in other regions of the world, the Brits used boundaries to divide and conquer. The Brits made the border between Afghanistan and Pakistan, known as the Duran line, go through Pashtunistan. The British-drawn border is why Pakistan is now such an important consideration in any effort to manage Afghanistan. The Taliban (Pashtuns) are very connected to land that is within Pakistan. This is like the Kurdistan problem between Iraq, Turkey, Syria and Iran and the Hutsi and Tutus tribal areas that cross Zaire and Rwanda's British-made borders. Poorly placed lines on a map can create big problems.

But even an empire that shaped much of the world through successful diplomatic, military and commercial endeavors was no match for the land in between. The Brits suffered three humiliating defeats in three Afghan campaigns. The current effort in Afghanistan is their fourth entry. One Afghan officer told me "the Afghans hate the British and would no sooner kill them all except that they are here as your (the United States') guests, so we tolerate their presence."

In the years after World War II, the Soviet Union and the United States competed for the hearts and minds of the "third" world, seeking to deny the other influence in any given place. The Soviet Union poured resources into its Afghan neighbor more heavily than the United States. The Afghans gladly took what they could from those who came bearing gifts. Like the Brits before them, the Russians started their efforts to influence Afghanistan in the capital, Kabul, and worked their way outward. For a few decades, Kabul had recognizable prosperity and government institutions, including an army, that resembled those of a sovereign nation. However, the same power base Churchill identified in the 1800s as the source of uprising against the Brits and any economic progress the British intrusion brought, began exerting their influence on the people against the Communist-backed government in Kabul. This force was made up of illiterate and influential elders who were positioned as mullahs (religious leaders). Churchill referred to some of them as Talibs.[1]

On the heels of the 1979 religious uprising in Iran that saw the Ayatollah Khomeini's followers expel the U.S.-backed Shah and seize the U.S. Embassy, the Soviet Russians invaded Afghanistan — not for Afghanistan's roses, opium, fruits or goats, but to protect Soviet prestige from a religious-based assault on the USSR's Cold War investment. They also may have sought to halt the spread of the Islamic uprising into Soviet satellites bordering Afghanistan.

The 1980s saw the Reagan Doctrine, a form of Truman Doctrine on steroids, mobilize the United States' clandestine services to support the Afghans as the enemy of our enemy - a concept that is well known in southwest Asia. With that, another world power found itself in a campaign, albeit dark and secret, in the land in between — not for what was in Afghanistan but as a move in a broader chess game. The U.S. began funneling weapons and money through Pakistan to holy warriors, like Osama

---

1 The Malakand Field Force 1897, W.L Spencer Churchill, The Project Gutenburg EBook of the Story of the Malakand Field Force, Edition 10, page 8.

Bin Laden, with little thought to the moves that would come into play later. My fourth grade teacher, Mrs. Ross, once invoked Confucius during class, saying: "Do not use a wild tiger to get rid of a rabid dog because you will then be stuck with a wild tiger!" The wild tiger used to expel the Soviets from Afghanistan flew airplanes into our landmark buildings.

After almost a decade of wasting lives and resources in Afghanistan, the Soviet Union withdrew in 1989. With the Soviets vanquished, the U.S. quickly lost interest in Afghanistan. The Soviet-mentored government of Afghanistan began to unravel within two years. In a centuries-old tradition, the Khans amassed networks of fighters mostly along tribal lines in a struggle to control as much of Afghanistan as their might and influence might allow. The fighting was brutal, with stories of sport decapitations, cannibalism by trickery, rape and genital mutilation. There was no rule of law, only the law of the gun and endless fighting and killing.

In the 1990s, Pakistan wanted to make sure Afghanistan would not be ruled by a group aligned with Pakistan's neighbor and mortal enemy, India. While the Northern Alliance had an affinity for India, the conservative Muslim tribe of Pashtuns was Pakistan's greatest hope for influence, given that Pashtunistan lay in both Afghanistan and Pakistan. By the mid-1990s, with mentoring and assistance from Pakistan's Inter-Services Intelligence, also known as the ISI (Pakistan's version of the U.S. Central Intelligence Agency), the Taliban fought their way to power, gaining acceptance from the people by providing a rough, but easily understood, Sharia justice system. Rough justice is better than no justice.

While most of the world shunned the Taliban government of Afghanistan, two groups embraced them: Pakistan and Al Qaeda, led by former CIA darling, Osama Bin Laden. In a scene reminiscent of Godfather II when the Mafia bosses celebrated their arrangement with the government of Cuba, Osama Bin Laden, who had been expelled from his native Saudi Arabia and later Sudan, found a country that would give his organization sanctuary to rain terror on the world of atheists and non-believers.[2]

In the late 1990s, both India and Pakistan demonstrated to the world that they had acquired nuclear weapons. In 1998, Al Qaeda blew up two U.S. embassies. President Bill Clinton ordered an attack using dozens of cruise missiles with the intent to kill Osama Bin Laden at one of his training camps in Afghanistan. Shortly before the attack, to avoid risking a nuclear exchange between Pakistan and India, the U.S. advised Pakistan of the attack so they would not think India had launched missiles at Pakistan.[3] Osama Bin Laden fled the targeted camp minutes before the missiles hit.

The American people, media and Congress had little appreciation for what had just taken place because they were fixated on President Bill Clinton's dalliance with a female intern. The cruise missile attack was dismissed by many political leaders and the media as a pathetic attempt to divert attention from the sexual scandal. Al Qaeda struck again in late 2000, with a suicide boat-borne explosive device killing 17 and wounding 39 sailors on the USS Cole.

On Sept. 9, 2001, Al Qaeda suicide bombers posing as international reporters tricked the legendary anti-Taliban Tajik leader of the Northern Alliance, Ahmad Shah Massoud, into taking an interview. Armed with a camera full of explosives, the "reporters" blew themselves up, killing the one leader Bin Laden knew would be sought by the CIA as an ally after the attacks he was planning for two days later. A prime suspect in the betrayal is a Pashtun named Abdul Rasul Sayyaf. A warlord with strong ties to the anti-Western Wahhabi radical Muslims of Saudi Arabia, Sayyaf is currently a power broker in the Afghan Parliament.

---

2 Osama Bin Laden referred to those who did not believe in any God as atheists, such as the Soviet Union and Saddam Hussein who believed only in himself. He referred to Christian believers as non-believers because they believed in false prophets.

3 National Commission on Terrorist Attacks Upon the United States, Chapter 4. www.9-11comission.gov/report/911Report_Ch4.htm

In the days after 9-11, the CIA and U.S. Special Operations forces deployed to Afghanistan with pallets of cash to befriend the enemies of America's enemy: the warlords that made up the Northern Alliance. The U.S. strategy was to quickly topple the Taliban; capture or kill Osama Bin Laden; then, find and move onto the Bush administration's "real" objective: Saddam Hussein and Iraq. There was little thought of how U.S.-enriched Afghan warlords might impede the development of institutions that could sustain an stable Afghan nation-state that would deny a haven to Al Qaeda.

Weeks into the war, Pakistan asked for a moratorium on the final crush of the Taliban so it could extract their ISI intelligence agents. The U.S. agreed. We helped our ally airlift not only operatives, but also their Taliban friends, some of whom would later command the resurgence of the Taliban and other forces hostile to the U.S.-led coalition.[4]

The U.S. was a member of NATO, the North Atlantic Treaty Organization, a collection of countries that came together by treaty in 1949 in response to the threat of the Soviet Union against European nations. The treaty declares in Article 5 that an attack on any member nation is an attack on all member nations. When Al Qaeda, led by Osama Bin Laden in Afghanistan, attacked the United States on September 11, 2001, the United States asked NATO to invoke Article 5, which is why NATO is operating in Afghanistan today.[5]

With the Mullah Omar's Taliban and Bin Laden's Al Qaeda on the run, the U.S. turned its attention to Iraq for the next seven years. The U.S.

---

4 Ahmed Rashid, Descent into Chaos: The United States and the Failure of Nation Building in Pakistan, Afghanistan, and Central Asia, Viking Adult (2008)

5 NATO continues to exist despite the breakup of the Soviet Union and its Warsaw Pact which was an alliance of communist nations. The Warsaw Pact nations, such as Poland and Slovakia were considered nations held against their people's will behind the Soviet's "Iron Curtain," a term coined by Winston Churchill. Many former Warsaw Pact nations are now members of NATO. NATO's most recent operation was in Libya in 2011 to overthrow Qaddafi. The operation involved neither European territory nor an attack on a member nation.

left behind in Afghanistan a small military force and financial aid modest by today's standards, but enormous from the perspective of a place mired in the 14th century. The U.S. also left in place a Pashtun named Karzai to establish a stable pro-western government in Kabul. Pakistan continued to hedge its bets, helping the U.S. with logistics but continuing its dark support of the Taliban and Al Qaeda. Karzai did what an Afghan leader does — he shared the spoils of his position with the warlord Khans, who have been and continue to command power through a combination of fear, respect, and newly found wealth in the form of United States dollars that were recklessly thrown about the land in between.

This was the shadowy network that awaited me and all the other men and women who deployed to Afghanistan to do good things in defense of their nation's security.

Landlocked Afghanistan © iStock

CHAPTER 2:

APPRECIATION, EMBARKATION, TRANSFORMATION AND INTEGRATION- BECOMING A PART OF SOMETHING BIG

"Just as a body, though one, has many parts,
but all its many parts form one body."

1 Corinthians 12:12

In late February 2010, after much preparation for my tour of duty, farewell parties and personnel actions at my civilian job, the Army called off my mission because of a mistake by a staff officer who "turned off" or eliminated the legal trainer positions, including the one I was to fill. Days later, word came from Afghanistan to stand by because a fix was in the works. From outside the military, my family, friends and co-workers wondered, "What the hell is going on? Can this Army make up its mind? Why do you put up with this?" Word came that the issue was fixed and I was to report on April 2, 2010. Days before my report date, it was pushed back a week to April 9. Days before April 9, there still were no orders. Then just 48 hours before my new report date, the uncertainty ended when an email arrived with my orders attached. From conversations with many reservists, I know that mine was one of the more stable experiences in going from reserve to active status in support of war.

I headed to the airport carrying a few extra pounds from all the goodbye lunches, dinners, drinks and parties given by friends, not to celebrate, but to spend some time with someone they feared they may not see again. The airport goodbyes were as hard as you can imagine. That last hug would pop into my head from time to time in the year that followed, my heart racing at the thought that the hug might be the last I would have with my daughter. As quickly as it would pop into my head, I would do my best to shut it out.

On a layover in Philadelphia International Airport, I checked out the USO lounge. It is an impressive facility that provides cash-strapped young soldiers and their families with hot food, cold drinks, phone, internet access, and a comfortable place to rest on unimaginably long journeys. Most Americans know the USO as the organization that brings notable entertainers to the troops serving in hostile fire zones. Run by volunteers and entirely privately funded by big-hearted Americans, the USO is the closest thing in this world to an absolute good.

Boarding the flight to Atlanta, the flight attendant put me in first class. As the plane left the gate, the hum of the engines and the comfort of the admiral's chair sent me into a slumber. Awakening to the sound of "Sir! Sir!," a young man shattered my joy. Mechanical problems had brought the plane back to the gate an hour after I fell asleep. The young man, an Air Force Academy grad, continued the public outpouring of appreciation and offered to buy me a beer while the mechanics worked on the plane for the next hour. We deplaned with the rest of the passengers and made our way to the bar. Sometimes a good deed goes sour. We later watched dumb founded as our plane pulled away from the gate with our luggage and carry-ons aboard. We had missed the re-boarding announcement. The young man turned to me and said somberly, "Sir, we screwed you."

US Airways put us onto the next flight to Atlanta. As we boarded, distressed at the fate of our carry-ons, another flight attendant took me by the hand and sat me down in first class. In a heavy Hungarian accent, she told me her son was a Marine serving in Afghanistan. When she learned of the separation from our carry-ons, she sprang into action and had the pilots call ahead to make contact with the crew of the earlier plane. Our bags would be waiting for us on arrival, she pledged. She gave me a hug as I deplaned and asked me to contact her son when I got to Afghanistan. It's a promise I kept.

The next morning, a Saturday, I arrived at the much-maligned CONUS Replacement Center ("CRC") in Fort Benning, Georgia. So infatuated is the Army with acronyms, that it has acronyms that include acronyms. CONUS stands for Continental United States. CRC is a camp where soldiers, Department of Defense civilians and contractors who were deploying as individuals to Iraq and Afghanistan spend a week getting equipped, medically vetted and minimally trained for their destination. Soldiers deploying with their unit did not go through the CRC. The layout of the camp is eerily similar to that of Dachau, the Nazi concentration camp near Munich.

A non-commissioned officer (a.k.a. sergeant) instructed the group to leave our bags by a pole and move to the briefing tent several hundred yards away. Reluctantly, we left our bags at the pole as instructed and proceeded to the briefing tent. We sat down and a big burly senior non-commissioned officer forcefully narrated the first slide of our briefing: "In a transient unit, as this, theft is common place. So don't leave your belongings alone for a second or they will be gone." A chaplain and I looked at each other in disbelief at the contradictory instructions and we sighed. It was at that moment that it hit me hard: "You're in the Army now - again!" I later learned that someone had taken the chaplain's bag containing bibles and sermons and other materials. He never saw the bag again.

The camp population was roughly half military and half civilian, the great majority of which was deploying to Afghanistan and Iraq. Some were headed for Sudan, Egypt and Kuwait. Military personnel were mostly senior officers and noncommissioned officers going to special assignments to replace individuals. Some were surgeons, including one who specialized in amputations, along with veterinarians, computer intelligence specialists, lawyers. I met a young captain who had given birth to a child just six months earlier. I would see her often over the next year at Camp Eggers where she was the headquarters company commander. The contractor population was a quilt of skilled and unskilled personnel, including lawyers, accountants, mapping specialists, linguists, cafeteria workers, security guards and drivers. Many hoped the high-paying, low-skill risky jobs in a dangerous far-away land would allow them to save their homes from the epic wave of foreclosures sweeping America.

Folks were on their own in the evenings. We gathered at the gazebos that peppered the camp, smoking cigarettes and cigars, drinking beer and sharing stories. Many of the contractors were former military personnel with tales of deployments to Iraq or Afghanistan when they were soldiers or marines.

One man in particular was especially entertaining — a lively Latino. A heavy-set Puerto Rican with a plump, squarish face with a slight beard, dark hair and eyes, I first came across him in line for chow at the dining facility (DFAC). He asked the server for some pork and beans. The elderly lady replied, "You don't eat that." In a high-pitched Bronx voice, he responded, "What do you mean I don't eat this? Look at my belly! Do I look like I don't eat this?!" The server warned him that the dish contained pork. "Lady, I am not Muslim, I am Puerto Rican!" he exclaimed.

Later, the lively Latino was holding court in a gazebo. He was describing his top bunkmate, who had an aversion to bathing and who farted while he snored. While in bed below, he heard his bunkmate speaking in Polish to his wife on the phone. "I don't know what he was saying. I just know he starts to speak deeper and lower, repeating some word over and over again! Then the bed starts to vibrate! This guy has no shame! At least I take it into the bathroom and have my Skype session with my wife in the stall. Man, I just get that laptop on one knee and lean it against the stall door and baby, we are in business!" From there, the discussion went downhill. Bed was the better alternative, despite the constantly slamming doors that kept postponing a good night's sleep.

If you have seen a war movie or two, you can imagine what our days were like as we got ready for war. Buses moving people from place to place so you can wait in various lines to get equipment, fire-resistant uniforms, weapons, immunizations, medical, dental, legal and financial screenings. There were many interesting people to meet during the long waits. One was an Afghan-born interpreter whose family moved to Denver when he was a young boy. A Hazara, his father chose Denver because of its changing seasons and its similar altitude to Kabul, which also has snow-capped mountains. He was excited about his pending job as a contract interpreter. His grandmother in Herat had arranged for him to meet and marry an Afghan girl. He would get to see his brother, who had been working as an interpreter for a couple of years. He was going to draw a salary of more than $210,000 per year. Of course, the contractor that employed him was charging the U.S. taxpayers much more than $210,000 for the service. A contrasting but equally interesting story was that of an Iraqi native, a former interpreter, now an active duty U.S. Army soldier. He was on his way to serve his adopted country in his native country on the annual salary of a Grade 4 Junior enlisted soldier. His salary? $22,668 per year. He was truly inspirational.

By Thursday afternoon, I had qualified medically and scored expert firing my weapon on the range. The Indian Guides marksmanship training I got at age five in Pine Forrest Camp, Shohola, PA was still paying dividends. I was eager to get on the Freedom Flight to Southwest Asia and begin my wartime service to the nation. I had spent the night before cramming $6,000 of equipment into four duffle bags and carefully packing my carry-on so it would fit precisely into the available space.

Then a rumor so ridiculous it had to be true, started to spread among the troops. A volcanic eruption in Iceland might cancel our flight to Kuwait.

It turned out that a cloud of volcanic dust over Europe was threatening airplane traffic with engine failures. The cadre of military trainers moved us to the airfield on a sliver of hope that we might get out. Or, maybe it was a pacifying white lie to get us to the field in an orderly fashion. Our duffels were loaded up and our carry-ons were carefully inspected by K-9 soldiers. Then we were told that our flight was cancelled and that we may not deploy for another week. Hundreds of us were locked down in the air terminal like prisoners, sleeping on cots, eating "Jimmy Deans" boxed lunches, and worse, subject to the dreaded General Order Number 1: no alcohol. The days did not fly by that week. It was reminiscent of the movie "Groundhog Day." Every morning, I would wake up to find myself still at Fort Benning and still in a large hangar with 300 of my closest friends.

During my captivity, I overheard an older man use the experience to counsel a young, engaged doctor on what he could expect from his pending nuptials:

> You like livin' the way we've been livin' at the airfield? Then you gonna like married life 'cause that's what it's like. You be told when to get up, when and where you can go, what time you gots to come back, when you can shower, what you can buy and when you can drink. In fact, you like how we had no hot water here all week? That's what being married is like cause she gonna use up all the hot water all the time!

Another doctor I met was planning her wedding, which was to take place upon her return from her pending deployment. It would be her second marriage. Her pending deployment to Afghanistan was her third tour. Her first husband divorced her when she deployed on her second.

Broken families are another casualty of war and too common for soldiers who have been on multiple deployments. The Army has a force generation cycle that gives a soldier at least one year at home in between deployments. Those I have talked to have said it is far less time than it sounds. Much of the time at "home" is actually spent away at schools or in the field training for the next deployment. The stress on the force is enormous and it has shown in divorce rates and suicides. In 2008, the Army had a record year for suicides. In 2009, the rate doubled that of 2008. In 2010, the 2009 record was broken.

On Sunday, I awoke in a field of green string beans as far as I could see – rows of soldiers wrapped up in General Issue (GI) sleeping bags. Georgia can get surprisingly chilly on an April morning. The Army chaplains, having recovered from the theft of a bag full of sermons, held service in the flight briefing room. "When we are delayed, it's because God knows we are not quite ready." In an obvious reference to the frustration we felt by the volcanic delay, Chaplain Phillips recounted his long-delayed journey to become an officer in the Army. The sermon brought me back seven years to when I was angry with God for not letting me deploy with my buds because I was stricken with an old man's cancer. It took me a year to get over that anger, with some help from my daughter, Julie. Some school children sent her a box of Christmas toys because they thought her daddy was in Iraq that Christmas of 2003. When my daughter realized why these toys came in the mail, she said she was glad I was home and not in Iraq. That was the moment I stopped feeling sorry for myself, realizing that there were thousands of men and women overseas wishing they could have what I had at that moment —holiday time at home with family.

I was delayed but not deterred. I knew that this would soon pass and I would proceed with my mission. I would deploy not with a unit, but as an individual replacement. Still, I would not be alone. I hoped to God I was ready.

The week in the hangar featured excursions to the gym, the Post Exchange (PX), which is similar to a small-scale mall with a food court, department store and smaller hobby shops, the Post Theater, a bowling alley and the Infantry Museum. We were under strict controls, moving from place to place by bus. We could not leave the premises of wherever we were until the bus returned. On one trip to the bowling alley, a contractor was picked up by a woman for what older folks might call an "afternoon delight," the younger ones a "booty call." Somehow, the cadre got word and waited for his return to the bowling alley. He was quickly whisked to headquarters and expelled from CRC, thereby terminating his ability to deploy. The booty call cost the man his job.

On a trip to the Infantry Museum, I had the honor and pleasure to meet Hal Moore, hero of the Battle of Ia Drang Valley, South Vietnam in November of 1965. He was played by Mel Gibson in the movie, "We Were Soldiers." In an act that might be called artistic license, Hollywood dropped the last three words from the title of General Moore's book "We Were Soldiers Once and Young." I would call that unfortunate, artistic butchery. Most Americans are far removed from war, by geography and degrees of separation. Even when America was embroiled in two simultaneous wars in Afghanistan and Iraq, less than 1% of the American population was in military service. From that distance, soldiers, standing tall, uniformed and equipped to take America's fight to its enemies, are larger than life men and women, professionals on the job. Get closer to them and you will be in awe at the youth of these professionals. Even aged veterans like me get startled when we see young children heading into harm's way, especially since I've raised a few children of my own.

One young soldier at the hangar during volcano week caught my eye and tugged at my heart. The soldier slept with a replica of Woody from Disney's "Toy Story" and a blankie. During the day I noticed the soldier lovingly place Woody in a sitting position by his blue blankie. His comrades gave him no grief. He was young enough to have been a small boy when "Toy Story" first hit the big screen and old enough to have a toddler that could have given Woody and his blanket to his young daddy to keep him company while in harm's way. It was heartwarming and gut wrenching to me either way. I wish war-fighting could be left to old farts like me.

One night, a voice mail appeared on my cell. The message was from my wife: "I just watched a show on PBS about Afghanistan and pedophilia. Sick! You are about to go to one strange place." I found the Frontline episode online and, using a set of headphones, I learned of Bacha Bazi, a term for pre-adolescent boys who are bought by powerful men and used for dancing, serving tea and sexual amusement.[6] It was a topic I would soon learn that Afghans were uncomfortable discussing. When the subject was broached, it was often in the context of some powerful warlord or high-level government official.

After one full week of delay, we got word that a plane was on its way to Benning to pick us up for the long flight to Kuwait. A young chaplain led a Christian service, reminding us that we were ambassadors for Jesus, that if we performed our mission with mercy in our hearts, the world would notice and then envy us for our exceptional demeanor, one that is not of ordinary men. He then handed out a tactical communion set: a shot-glass shaped plastic container with two layers separated by foil. I peeled away the top layer of foil to reveal a Catholic-style wafer of unleavened bread. I broke it and ate it. Then, I peeled the second layer of foil to expose grape juice - no wine. Even Jesus' word did not pull rank on General Order Number 1.

We assembled in Freedom Hall. The CRC Battalion Commander, a small African-American woman, sang the National Anthem in an explosive voice that made it clear that she had sung in church while growing up in South Carolina. It was a very moving moment as she belted out the almost impossible high notes while we all stood at attention, saluting the immense American flag on the wall, knowing we were finally going into harm's way for our Nation. I made last-minute calls to my wife and each of

---

6 As of the date of this writing, the episode is still available online at http://www.pbs.org/wgbh/pages/frontline/dancingboys/?utm_campaign=homepage&utm_medium=bigimage&utm_source=bigimage

my children. I could only leave voicemails for my girls. Julia was in school and her phone was off. Jackie did not answer her phone, neither did my mom.

We sat for what seemed like hours in the briefing room before being called to board the plane. They called out the last name and rank of the soldier, who responded with the last four numbers of his ID number. "Jones!" "5555!" First, the Flight Officer in Charge (OIC), Colonel Jones (a petite female veterinarian); then the Flight Non-Commissioned-Officer In-Charge (NCOIC); then the colonels. I was the third colonel called, the fifth person to walk to the enormous plane parked alone about 500 yards from the terminal. The two colonels who boarded before me were doctors heading to a Forward Operating Base outside of Kabul. One was a tabbed Army Ranger and orthopedic surgeon from Wisconsin who specialized in extremities and amputations. He served in Iraq during the surge and was sadly quite busy. He had told me he hoped to be bored during this surge. The other was a Special Forces tabbed Vietnam War veteran and surgeon who went to medical school later in his career. We both knew some of the same Special Forces officers who had served in the Tenth Special Forces Group.

It was a bright, sunny, cloudless day as we strutted to the plane in a single column in the order we were called, each of us toting our one, carefully measured carry-on. I wished we could take a picture, but we had been sternly warned that Operational Security (OPSEC) prohibited photography. We then walked up the long mobile stairs to one of the many doors of the DC-10 and boarded. As the crew got the tired, but hopefully airworthy, plane ready for takeoff, they announced that the VCR was broken so they would not be able to show us the episode of "Cheers" that they had lined up. I thought, "VCR? 'Cheers?' God please just keep this ole plane in the air!" Just before 3 p.m., the plane started to move. Within a minute, we were airborne. No taxiing for this flight.

We flew about two and a half hours to Bangor, Maine, where we landed to refuel. We were greeted by the Maine Troop Greeters, a group about whom PBS did a documentary. It was yet another moving moment in my journey. Some of the greeters were Vietnam, Korean and World War II veterans and their wives, dressed in red, white and blue. After several hours, and a lobster roll, we re-boarded the plane and started off for Rota, Spain. When we landed, our bodies said it was 2 a.m. Spain's morning sun beat down on us as we walked to the terminal for what turned out to be a painful four-hour layover. We finally re-boarded and started the last leg of our journey to the Kuwait air base, catching a glimpse of Mount Ararat on the Armenian-Turkish border, where Noah's Ark is believed to have landed centuries ago. We arrived in Kuwait at 11 p.m. Saturday night, local time, but it was 4 p.m. Eastern Body Time!

A convoy of buses provided a 90-minute ride to Ali al Salaam, a U.S. Army base that serves as America's traffic control for U.S. Army and Marine troops coming and going to Iraq and Afghanistan. The curtains stayed closed for the duration of the ride to minimize reminders to the Kuwaiti people that Americans were in their midst. We arrived after midnight and were assigned tents in which to sleep. The Kuwaiti government, which had been saved from enslavement to Saddam Hussein by U.S. blood and resources twenty years earlier, won't allow the U.S. to build permanent barracks for its troops.

About four hours later, 6 a.m. local time, I was headed for my flight to Afghanistan. Ali al Salaam was bustling with movements of large numbers of Marines on their way to Bastogne Air Base to join the fight that had been raging in Afghanistan's Helmand Province for months. It is adjacent to Camp Leatherneck, the huge Marine base in southwestern Afghanistan where some of the heaviest fighting takes place.

Criss-crossing the Marines' path were Screaming Eagles, the soldiers of the historic 101st Airborne Division. The Screaming Eagles were making their way to Kandahar for yet another battle to keep the Taliban from Mullah Omar's birthplace. There was a feeling of bigness and of history as the sun beat down on us, raising the temperature to almost 100 degrees Fahrenheit before 9 a.m.

We boarded buses, curtains drawn of course, and made our way to the C-17 that would take us on a four-hour flight to Bagram Air Base northeast of Kabul. At cruising altitude, we were allowed to shed our flak jackets, ballistic eye protection and helmets. After listening to a concert on my iPod using noise-canceling headphones, I walked over to an exit door with a small glass portal to get my first glimpse of the land that has been at the crossroads of so much conflict for so long. I thought I was looking at the mountains of the moon, far reaching and barren. Then snow-capped mountains began to appear, and this, I guessed, might be the beginnings of the Hindu Kush range. I snapped photographs of the peaks and valleys below, able to make out the walled-in structures of villages. Then word came to prepare for landing, which meant donning body armor, helmets, eye protection and leather gloves. After a few minor evasive maneuvers, routine in hostile fire areas, we were on the ground in the land in between.

We lined up, facing the rear of the plane in two lines. The hydraulics whined, lifting the back doors open from top to bottom, exposing a breath-taking view of the snow-capped mountains, reminiscent of the Colorado Rockies. I led one line of soldiers out of the plane and across the runway into a plywood briefing room where the only thing I remember hearing was a casual comment the sergeant made about the water:

Welcome to Afghanistan. Here we drink bottled water. Make sure you check your bottle carefully before drinking, because the locals like to spit in them and put them back as new for you and me to drink.

Our mission was going to be harder than I had imagined.

CRC

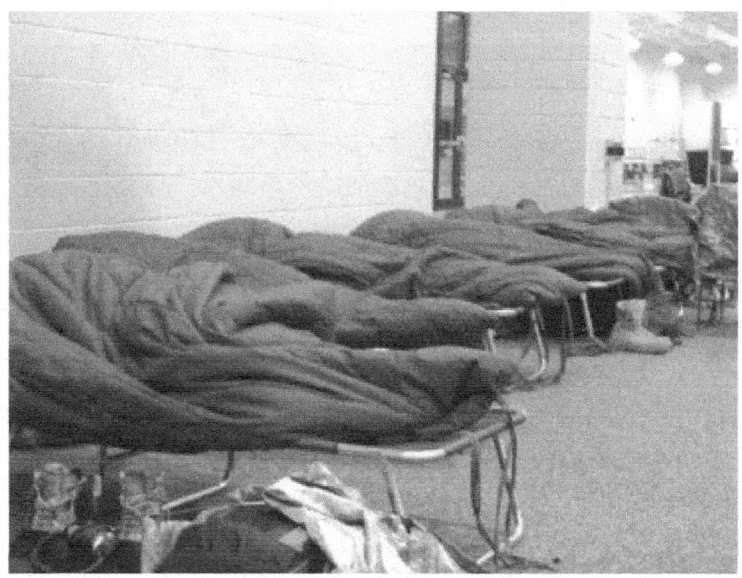

Sleeping String Beans

Woody Goes to War.

I still get chills thinking about standing at attention and saluting this flag to the National Anthem moments before leaving for the Middle East.

Freedom Flight to Kuwait, weapons and all.

The Famed Maine Troop Greeters at our first three-hour layover.

A painful 4-hour layover in Rota Spain

Mount Ararat

100 Degree morning in Kuwait - rise and shine

C-17 to Afghanistan

Hindu Kush Mountain Range

CHAPTER 3:

ICE CREAM EVERY DAY

"To everything there is a season, and a time to
every purpose under the heaven."

Ecclesiastes 3:1

Bagram was the largest U.S. base in Afghanistan. It was once a key base for the Soviets during their fateful decade-long blood and treasury-letting war. Today, it was a scene of quick farewells to the surgeons with whom I had spent the last two weeks. I grabbed a hot cup of coffee at the Patrick Tillman USO nearby, studying the Tillman memorabilia while a liaison officer arranged a ride for me to Kabul. The USO was named in honor of Pat Tillman, the NFL star and genuine hero who, motivated by the attacks of 9-11, gave up his multi-million-dollar career to serve his nation as an Army Ranger. He died at the hands of his comrades through the fog of war known as friendly fire. The tragedy was exacerbated into a storm of controversy when General McCrystal's command recklessly reported to his family and his nation that he died by enemy fire — something known to be false seconds after Tillman perished. A variation on the theme of friendly fire known as "Green on Blue," where Afghan soldiers and police would kill American soldiers, would become a haunting reality in the coming year for my brothers and sisters serving in the Coalition.

One of the dining facilities (DFAC) on Bagram served up my first meal in Afghanistan. Typical American cafeteria fare, the food was actually pretty good – a surprise that would be repeated at every U.S. base I frequented during my tour. The same could not be said at the International Security Assistance Force (ISAF) Headquarters, which serves as the supreme command of all NATO forces in Afghanistan, or at the ISAF Joint Command (IJC) Headquarters, which serves as command for NATO fighting forces. Those dining facilities were run by European contractors - vive la différence? Forget about it! I often overheard GIs from ISAF and IJC heap joyous praise on the fare they ate at Camp Eggers, which would be my base camp during my deployment. As I finished my first meal and contemplated dessert, I recalled the admonishment of a high school classmate, now a Marine Colonel, to resist the daily temptations of the ice cream bar. I succumbed to the temptation that day but assured myself that ice cream would be an occasional treat, not something worth threatening my waistline and health by overindulgence.

The liaison officer got me on a flight full of Navy personnel who made room for an old Army Colonel for an unremarkable, 10-minute flight to Kabul International Airport. Waiting for the last leg of my trip to Camp Eggers, with nothing but new faces and places to see, a Navy Lieutenant, Rebecca Gels, smiled and said hello. Also newly arrived in country, she was a forensic accountant deployed to assist the funding, training, equipping and supplying of the Afghan National Army's medical system. My civilian experience includes working closely with forensic accountants and lawyers investigating embezzlement schemes. Perhaps it was divine providence or serendipity that we were on the same plane. Our paths would cross again months later when we instigated a significant shake-up of a corrupt medical supply network – a shake-up that seemed to upset some U.S. leaders as much as the Afghan profiteers.

Two Chevy Suburbans arrived for the ride to Eggers. Each one was equipped with bullet-proof glass, armored plates, and radio-jamming antennas to block cell phones, garage door openers and car key remotes that might trigger roadside bombs. Completely exhausted, but pumped with adrenalin, we made our way through the city streets of Kabul, at once looking for suspicious activity but also taking in the sites: bustling bazaar commerce, old bearded men drinking tea in front of run-down stores loaded with junk that would make Sanford & Son proud, sides of lamb and fowl hanging outside, little boys scrambling about and women clad in blue burkas holding the hands of their little girls – a tableau of Afghan life playing out in clouds of dust kicked up by what seemed like thousands of Toyotas, the vehicle of choice.

Our caravan made its way around Massoud Circle and through a check-point into the Green Zone where the U.S. Embassy, ISAF Headquarters, the Afghan Ministry of Defense, the Presidential Palace and Camp Eggers were located. Camp Eggers, once an upscale neighborhood populated by the King's relatives and diplomats, was now the cramped, maze-like headquarters of the NATO Training Mission – Afghanistan (NTM-A) and the Combined Security Transition Command - Afghanistan (CSTC-A).

NTM-A's mission is to recruit, equip and train the Afghan National Army and the Afghan National Police, a heavily armed police force, and to develop their ministries. CSTC-A is the U.S. entity that pays for it all, at a cost of $1 billion U.S. dollars each month. This sum excludes the $9 billion a month the U.S. spends on its own military and State Department personnel and operations dedicated to Afghanistan.

The old primitive Afghan homes on Camp Eggers were now offices to NTM-A/CSTC-A. Shipping containers, called "conexes," were dropped in every available space and converted to offices and sleeping quarters. The U.S. leases the old homes from prominent Afghan government leaders at rates ranging from $5,000 to $8,000 a month each. Gouging the U.S. was the least the Afghan power brokers could do to support the U.S. led effort to rebuild Afghanistan - one of the poorest, most backward and war ravaged countries in the world. How backward you may ask? It was not uncommon to find rocks in and around the toilets at facilities built by the U.S. for the Afghans. "Why are there rocks in the toilet" was a question asked by some newly arrived coalition personnel. The answer: "because the Afghan soldiers were used to un-soiling themselves with rocks."

I arrived at my new home on a sunny, warm Monday at about 8 a.m. local time (still Sunday, 11:30 p.m. Fort Benning, Georgia, time, and God only knows what time it was inside my body clock.) For those stupid enough to have pulled an all-nighter in college or a night out on New York City, triple that feeling and you might come close to what it's like to travel nine and a half time zones over a span of 56 hours. A very-happy-to-see-me Colonel escorted me through the little camp that would soon become too familiar. I was his ticket home and he was not going to let anything bad happen to me. In a weekly ritual experienced by others before and after me, I went to the Monday afternoon synchronization meeting to meet the Afghan Army Development team led by Canadian Brigadier General David Neasmith and well represented by the U.S. Military Academy Class of 1986. The Army Development Team consisted of senior level Allied officers and contractors from varied military disciplines who were tasked with advising the Afghan National Army in the essential functions of a military such as operations, personnel, legal, medical, finance, intelligence, logistics, air operations, information systems, public affairs and more.

Despite the sleep deprivation, one point clearly sunk in as I was briefed by the multi-uniformed officers from around the world: the "fighting season" was fast approaching.

The concept of a fighting season was laid to waste by General Ulysses S. Grant in 1863 when, to the chagrin of Confederate General Robert E. Lee, Grant's engineers, infantry and artillery demonstrated they were willing to fight even when the seasonal weather did not cooperate.

However, this is Afghanistan, a land where it is solar year 1389, measured from the days Mohammed walked the Earth, but which looks stuck in the Christian year of 1389. When the mountain passes become impassable from snow and ice, the insurgents either lay down their arms to melt into the local population, or they head to the sanctuary of Pakistan. As spring approaches, they begin harvesting opium. Our briefers reported that the insurgents had completed the big harvest and had announced, through their surprisingly effective public relations arm, they would be greeting the U.S. surge with an offensive called al Fateh. They would be staging spectacular attacks and using money to buy off Afghan soldiers and police, who, in turn, would facilitate the bleeding of Coalition forces.

In early May, British Brigadier Levy sent an unclassified email complaining of an Afghan Army garrison commander of a base on the outskirts of Kabul whose corrupt and unruly behavior created an atmosphere that made Coalition troops in his command feel unsafe. On May 18, 2010, my crew and I loaded up two armored Sport Utility Vehicles and moved through Kabul to the Afghan Command and General Staff School. My Noncommissioned Officer-In-Charge conducted our movement briefing, explaining what to do in the event of breakdown or attack by small arms. I once asked Technical Sergeant Crowell what would happen if we ran into an Improvised Explosive Device (IED). His response was succinct: "Sir, then we're fucked." He was right, of course, but he followed up with the doctrinal answer: the surviving vehicle will call Force Protection or Movement Control and do its best to provide security and assistance to the disabled vehicle and its passengers until Force Protection (FORCEPRO) arrived.

We proceeded to our destination in full body armor, fire resistant uniforms, eye protection and leather gloves, pulling into the school at approximately 8:45 a.m. At that time, about ten kilometers away, a suicide bomber detonated his vehicle-borne bomb outside the entrance to the base that had been the topic of the British brigadier's email. It hit a convoy of coalition vehicles carrying senior personnel from the airport, having just arrived in country. Killed instantly were a Canadian and U.S. colonel, two U.S. lieutenant colonels, two U.S. senior noncommissioned officers and scores of Afghan women and children who were in a bus next to the doomed SUV.

The roads went "black," which meant all Coalition traffic was to stay at or get to the nearest Coalition or Afghan base and remain there while Force Protection did its job. So, we stayed locked down at the school.

As the hours passed, I looked at the watch on my right hand that was set to New York time. It was 3:30 a.m. Soon, my wife would be waking to begin her workday as a nurse. I knew she would listen to the early morning reports on the BBC. I began to think of the stress she would undergo, hearing of an attack in Kabul that killed American officers. If I could get to an internet-enabled computer, I might be able to send a text to her cellphone using the Verizon Wireless home page. But there was no internet access at the school. So, I waited with my comrades as we dined on local Afghan fare that our Canadian hosts had arranged for us. The killing hours in Afghanistan began at 6 a.m. and lasted until 11 a.m. That was when the insurgents conducted most of their attacks on coalition troops. It was a grisly phenomenon that remained true until I went home in March 2011[7]. Lunch became my favorite meal for the duration of my tour.

Finally, the roads went "amber," which meant we were allowed to proceed back to Camp Eggers with caution. Upon return to Camp Eggers, I immediately went to my quarters and accessed the internet service that costs a soldier $70 per month. Even after nine years in the country's capital, the Army still could not arrange free internet service like the Canadians provide for their troops in Kandahar. I sent a simple, nondescript text to my wife's cell phone: "Back on Base." It was now about 6 a.m. Eastern Time, 1530 (3:30 p.m.) Kabul time. My text arrived just as my wife made

---

7 In the spring of 2011, insurgents launched an attack at 6 pm Kabul time on the Intercontinental Hotel, holding it for many hours until U.S. Special Forces and airpower took it back.

her way to work with the BBC on the radio, which of course blurted out the news of the deadly attack on NATO forces in Kabul, Afghanistan.

Later that day, there was much consternation among the advisory team of Canadian, British and U.S. colonels. The official word was that the attacker had been tracked that morning by Afghan security forces, but they had lost him as he made his way through Kabul looking for a "random target of opportunity." The 10th Mountain Division convoy had reportedly been in the wrong place at the wrong time. The photograph of the doomed vehicle made it eminently clear that these six victims appeared before God instantly, with not a millisecond of apprehension. Those in the second car were wounded. The third vehicle contained stunned occupants that included the Staff Judge Advocate of the 10th Mountain Division. At Camp Eggers, I sat down with a Canadian officer who was a close friend of the deceased officer from Canada. A hint of water in his angry eyes, his deep personal anguish was apparent. We discussed Brigadier Levy's email. We wondered aloud if the attack on the 10th Mountain Division's headquarters element truly was random.

Over the next few months, I worked with my Afghan counterparts to investigate more allegations of corruption levied at the same Afghan garrison commander. It became clear to me that he was part of that class of men empowered and enriched by a mix of Afghan impunity and American largesse. Weak, barely responsive reports would come back from the Afghan investigators in response to allegations against this man. Before my tour was over, there was another suicide vehicle attack at the same spot. After I left, one of the most deadly attacks of the war on a NATO convoy took place at the same location.

That night on Skype, my wife was ever so grateful for the text. It came to her just as NPR had begun its BBC feed about the gruesome attack. Late-night for me, mid-afternoon for her, I told her I needed to get to sleep. I explained that, because I would be traveling all over Afghanistan to escort my Afghan general, I would be going to Bagram Air Base to trade in my older-generation body armor issued at Fort Benning for the more protective, second generation body armor system. She was all for me getting the better body armor, but wondered why the Army would issue second-rate equipment in the first place.

The following morning, a group of soldiers and contractors assembled at 5 a.m. on Gator Alley, the nickname for Camp Egger's main drag, to board the convoy of Mine Resistant Ambush Protected (MRAP) vehicles for the 90-minute trek to Bagram. MRAPs are large and desert brown. The soldiers call them Rhinos, a name which the operating crew hates. The crews prefer to call them Raptors. We buckled into the most uncomfortable seats ever designed by man. As we snaked through Kabul, cars did what they could to get as far away from our vehicles as fast as they could. No one wanted to be near potential targets of attack, especially after what happened the day before to the bus full of women and children. Some little children waved at our convoy and gave the thumbs up sign as we passed.

The gunner's swiveling turret made a constant clicking sound against the loud hum of our radio jammers as we roared through the streets, passing shops full of junk interspersed with colorful wedding reception halls. The convoy quickly hit open road, passing though the countryside of Afghanistan. Living compounds surrounded by thick hardened mud walls dotted the open plains against the beautiful backdrop of the Hindu Kush mountains. I wondered how many troops of the British and Soviet empires had witnessed the same sight over the centuries. Standing alongside a network of irrigation ditches, children continued to wave as we made our final approach, passing sheep herders and small shops before reaching the outer security perimeter of Bagram Air Base.

Suddenly, we came to a stop. The driver and commander of the convoy eventually dismounted my vehicle to see what was going on. They returned, excited, and spread the word to fellow crew members: We had driven into the tail end of an attack on the air base. "Dude, did you see that dead insurgent?" one soldier said to the other. "An Apache (helicopter gunship) ripped him apart!"

We waited while one of the crew members told his comrades about his pre-deployment exploits with a house full of strippers. It was amusing and annoying. There were no signs of rank on my body armor, and the young private didn't realize he had a colonel in his midst as he offered long, sordid details of extremities and reactions. With no women on board, and few others beside me and the crew, I made an internal command decision. While we sat through the clean-up of this attack, the MRAP would be a politically-correct-free zone. I looked at my eastern time zone watch. My wife was still sleeping through the Pennsylvania night. I wondered if I could get to the internet before she sipped her morning coffee with the BBC.

We were told that Bagram would be closed for business because Force Protection was in search of two or more potential insurgents at large on the base. The convoy's only duty now was to drop off those who were traveling through Bagram to begin their journey home for R&R (rest & relaxation) or for a joyous end of their tour of duty. Advised to keep our body armor on when dismounted and to "go red" – put a bullet in your weapon's chamber - we dropped off the fortunate travelers and headed back to Camp Eggers by way of Kabul International Airport. For the second straight day, I was able to send my wife a reassuring, if short, morning text: "Back at base."

The next day, I walked to the Ministry of Defense to meet with the Afghan legal generals. We drank green tea, ate yellow raisins and walnuts, and discussed plans for an upcoming trip to Kandahar. My Canadian JAG and I said our goodbyes and proceeded to walk back to base. As we walked, personnel at Camp Eggers tried to call us on the oversold Afghan wireless network, but they could not get through. They were trying to warn us that CJ2 (intelligence) had reported the presence of a suicide bomber in the Green Zone and that we were not to do exactly what we were doing — walk back to our offices from the Ministry of Defense. Making my way through security at Camp Eggers, I went straight to my office to find a broadcast email sent at the same time we had started back from the

Ministry, warning all not to walk through the Green Zone. After just three days in country, word quickly spread through the legal office at Camp Eggers: Don't travel with Colonel Carozza!

Days later, while meeting with General Neasmith and staff, his aide, a Canadian Infantry Captain, popped open the door to announce CJ2 was again reporting a suicide bomber trolling the Green Zone. Minutes earlier I had declined walking over to ISAF with a fellow Judge Advocate so I could attend this meeting. I tried reaching him on the Afghan wireless system. I tried to text him. Then the aide suddenly appeared again to announce that CJ2 believed the suicide bomber had made his way onto Eggers. Lieutenant Colonel Tom Tracy signaled to the aide to lock the conference room doors that led to the outside. A number of chuckles rose up in the room. The laughter evaporated when all realized the soundness of the idea and the severity of the news. The briefings continued until the captain returned to announce the base had been cleared. The news of the intrusion was declared a false alarm.

Just before my battlefield circulation to the large air base at Kandahar, word came of a combined rocket and ground assault on the base. One rocket hit near the Tim Horton's Coffee and Donut Shop, the Canadian equivalent of Dunkin' Donuts. If you want to piss off Canadians, take away their Tim Horton's after they have already been denied their beer! I declared to my legal advisory team that surely my luck had changed. This time, the lightning had struck before I arrived.

While in Kandahar, we traveled in a "soft" unarmored vehicle to and from the Coalition base and Camp Hero, home to the Afghan National Army's 205th Corps headquarters. As we made our way back onto the Canadian sector, we came upon a check point run by Slovakian guards. My driver forgot to tell us we were to all hold up our ID cards so the guards could inspect them using a telescope at a safe distance. We were not used to this procedure. At the bases in Kabul, cards were shown through the window as you came to the gate. We waited at the sign ordering us not to proceed until called forward. Then we waited some more.

The guards in the distance became restless and started waving their arms and shouting at us in words that we could not understand. My driver thought they were calling us forward and put the car in drive. In an instant, the guards raised their machine guns and prepared to open fire. I screamed at my driver to halt and he slammed on the brakes. The Slovakian guards continued to scream with their weapons aimed at us.

Soon, an armed Blackwater-looking guy came up to our side and yelled into our car: "What the fuck are you doing? Hold out your ID Cards so they can see them through their scope!" We pulled up to the understandably angry guards and listened to their mix of broken English and Slovakian. Just then, a hose from our vehicle's air conditioning compressor burst like a loud balloon, startling the guards and us.

When I got back to Camp Eggers, I sat outside the Green Bean Coffee shop, thinking about the different ways one can meet his Maker in this place. I started to think about what brought me here; why did I choose to be here? A lot of thoughts raced through my mind about my life journey leading me to this dangerous place, but one thing was overwhelmingly clear that night: while I am here, I am having ice cream every day.

Massoud Circle, outside of the Green Zone

The Afghan National Army Development Team, Canadian Brigadier General David Neasmith (front center right) and Sergeant Major Joseph Pedroza (front center left), Commanding. June 2010

Flags Lowered for 6 U.S. and Canadian Soldiers killed in May 18, 2010 Attack in Kabul

MRAPs getting ready to travel to Bagram on May 19, 2010

The Road to Bagram

Waiting for Force Protection to clean up after attack on base

Flags over Kandahar

CHAPTER 4:

YOU CAN'T GET THERE FROM HERE

"Faith is taking the first step even when you don't see the
whole staircase."

Dr. Martin Luther King, Jr.

Growing up in the mid-sixties for young boys meant a steady television diet of "Combat!," "Rat Patrol" and World War II movies galore.
Playtime in my Drexel Hill, Pennsylvania neighborhood had the boys taking sides and spreading out with their toy guns to begin the battle of the
day. The days were long and play was hard, crawling, hiding, and shooting
between the pre-World War II homes of this blue collar community and
waiting for medics to fix us up so we could fight again. Then came the
calls by mothers up and down the block, which meant the war was over - it
was dinner time. On some nights, as dinner was almost ready, there was
chatter on the television about a place called Vietnam. There were images
of American soldiers fighting and dying for real in a far-away land. A man

in a suit read the number of American soldiers and Marines killed that day versus the number of enemy forces killed, which was always many times more. Just what you would expect of the mighty U.S. Army. For many years, when asked "what do you want to be when you grow up?" the answer was easy — "a soldier!"

As the sixties became the seventies, interests expanded to baseball, football, hockey, music and girls. The war in Vietnam became more serious and confusing in the minds of young boys. There were protests, hair became longer; clothes brighter; and, eventually, the war that seemed a constant in adolescence came to a complete end as we became teenagers. There were scenes of helicopters tossed into the ocean from Navy ships after shuttling the last U.S. personnel away from that distant land that had caused so much pain, doubt and divisiveness in our country.

Another interest took hold in my life — a sense of right and wrong. Maybe it was a natural offshoot of my love for the Army — good guys beating bad guys; the Allies defeating the evil Nazis and the sadistic Japanese. Right needed might to make sure right could prevail, but right also needed to guide might.

In school, we watched a 16-mm film that showed some of the Japanese and German leaders prosecuted for crimes against humanity. It struck a chord with me. I was never a big Perry Mason fan, but the idea of right and wrong – the challenge of arguing for what was right — sparked my interest in the law. Eventually, I worked towards that goal. Despite a restlessness that often distracted me from the routine of study, I prepared for and mastered the Law School Admission Test and off to law school I went.

When I was in college and law school, the notion of military service was latent, forgotten in the post-Vietnam years as our military languished in spirit and reputation. However, time heals all wounds and President Reagan seemed to accelerate the cure, investing in both the spirit and equipping of the military during the eighties.

One afternoon, an unusual sight crossed my path in the halls of Villanova Law School: a Marine in a crisp looking uniform. The idea of combining two passions was intriguing. After a number of meetings with JAG recruiters from the Marines, Navy and Army, and bouncing the idea off older lawyers who looked fondly on their years in the service, I was sold on the idea of taking a different path.

Signing the dotted line brought thoughts of an uncertain future. It was a time of relative peace, clouded by the Cold War looming over the world. Where might this act of commitment to country take me? Most Americans probably never heard of Korea until Americans started fighting there in 1950. Likewise, few knew of or paid attention to Vietnam until President Lyndon Johnson sent hundreds of thousands of American boys to fight a war he promised would be fought by Asian boys. I figured if war did come while I was in uniform, it probably would be somewhere that most Americans couldn't find on a map. I began my military career on active duty and then migrated to a career in the Army Reserve, where I could pursue the private practice of law while maintaining a connection to service to nation.

Like most Americans before September 11, 2001, I thought little of Afghanistan. In 1979, when the Russians invaded Afghanistan, I remembered President Jimmy Carter with Congress in the cheering section threatening the Russians with the use of military force should they move toward the oil fields of Iran. There were scenes of anchorman Dan Rather making his way through the fabled Khyber Pass into Afghanistan with Mujahideen fighters, and images of the rebels shooting down Soviet MIG fighter jets with Stinger missiles supplied by the Central Intelligence Agency ("CIA").

Except for the reactivation of the Selective Service system requiring young men to register for the draft, these events meant little to young men in college and less to most other Americans. Years later, in the book "Blackhawk Down," author Mark Bowden mentioned that Osama Bin Laden, a darling of the CIA in the 1980s and resident in Afghanistan, had taught Somali tribal fighters to shoot down U.S. helicopters. There was disturbing news of the destruction of the thousand-year-old great Buddhist monuments in northern Afghanistan by a group of Islamic radicals known as "Talibs" or "students of the book." But all of that was a world away and of little matter to a young man struggling to juggle the competing demands of a civilian legal career, a military reserve career and a new family.

In August of 2001, while attending a Command and General Staff Course at Fort Dix, I confided in a chaplain about my gut-wrenching desire to resign my commission after fifteen years of service. I felt burned out from fifteen years of working two careers and missing weddings and other events with family because of military obligations. Imagine working long hours then telling your family you are taking some vacation time to go work a second job. That's what it had been like for too long.

The words of my five-year-old daughter kept haunting me: "Daddy, you always have to go away for the Army." The chaplain told me what he told other officers who came to him with similar concerns on almost a weekly basis: pray about it, give it a little time, look for that unmistakable sign and you will know what is right for you. That sign presented itself just a few weeks later on a horrible, sunny, blue-sky Tuesday in September. After picking up my three children from school, we spent the afternoon of that fateful day praying in church for the people who died and were dying in New York, Washington, DC and Pennsylvania.

I knew there would be military operations in Afghanistan to crush those who had terrorized the city where I was born and scarred the fields of the state my family called home. On September 12, I sent emails to officers I had trained with at the Tenth Special Forces Group to see if there was any way I could arrange for one of them to file a formal request that I be attached to them as a civil affairs specialist.

It was a long shot, or better said, wishful thinking. Those Special Forces operators were immediately hyper-focused on a new mission and they would not be taking reserve officers trained in Civil Affairs or otherwise. Years later, I saw one of the Special Forces officers in a "National

Geographic" feature on how Special Forces brought together the Northern Alliance to push the Taliban out of Afghanistan in just two months.

Almost a year after the 9-11 attacks, my chance to fight the war on terror came when a friend of mine with a Civil Affairs unit in Norristown, Pennsylvania told me about unusual training they had been conducting with the First Marine Expeditionary Force in California. From my position in an Army Reserve unit that specialized in preparing Reserve and Guard soldiers for activation and deployment, I knew the U.S. had been sending intel, medical and other support units to Kuwait during the summer of 2002, which would serve as a staging area for any move against Iraq. Members of the Bush administration insist the president did not make up his mind to invade Iraq until late 2002. My personal experience is that Bush and his team began preparing for the war in Iraq as early as June 2002, pulling resources and attention away from Afghanistan. Iraq was not Afghanistan. I had no illusions that Iraq had participated in or enabled the 9-11 attacks. Still, I transferred into the unit eager to serve with many friends I trained with for years.

I was reading the memoirs of Ulysses S. Grant at the time and two of his points stood out in my mind: The first was the need to leave large garrisons of troops behind to control territory and prevent the civilian population from quickly reconstituting the ability to wage war against your army. The second was that our nation usually gets its best service from those who wait for the call rather than from those who brashly seek the spotlight by volunteering. The latter point touched me personally as I wondered about my decision to step into a unit soon to be part of an invasion force. The former caught my attention because of the very public feud between Army planners and Secretary Donald Rumsfeld over the size of the invasion force.

Army Chief of Staff General Eric Shinseki told Congress of the need for 600,000 troops, not to conquer Iraq, but to effectively maintain stability after the fight. Shortly after his testimony, Secretary Rumsfeld essentially fired Shinseki, making him a lame duck by selecting his successor more than a year before Shinseki's term was over. The U.S. ended up invading Iraq with 100,000 troops, a number higher than what Rumsfeld wanted but as high as he would allow. The small force proved incapable of maintaining stability, allowing an insurgency to fester in Iraq that would consume our military for years to come.

As I pondered my personal decision and prepared with my brothers and sisters to be part of the spearhead of the invasion of Iraq with the 1st Marine Expeditionary Force, a different question began to dominate my thoughts: war or cancer. A routine private physical disclosed that I had a prostate specific antigen ("PSA") level of twelve, with four being a sign of cancer in men in their sixties. I was 42, an age where 2.5 would be cause for alarm. Several doctors assured me I most certainly did not have prostate cancer because of my young age, but acknowledged that the PSA was a concern. On a misty day at Fort Dix during training by the Special Operations University, my doctor gave me the news: a biopsy positive for cancer. I could not go forward with my unit to invade Iraq.

The night before that diagnosis, in a dream so vivid I could feel the morning air on my face, I stood tall and proud in the sun, dressed in the desert camouflage uniform given only to those deployed to the Middle East. But now I was stunned, being consoled by my friend who had just learned that he was selected for promotion to colonel. I would have served as his deputy in a Civil Affairs cell attached to the 1st Marine Expeditionary Force headquarters. At a time when he should have been elated, he stood by me somber as I stood stunned, mindlessly packing my things for a trip home. The reality that I would not be going hit hard. As I drove home that day, I needed to pull over because I could not see through my tears.

Maybe U.S. Grant was right. If I beat the cancer, I promised myself that I would wait to be called.

CHAPTER 5:
THE DEFECTIVE ARMY GENE AND THE URGE TO SERVE

"And I'll say to myself, 'You have plenty of grain laid up
for many years. Take life easy; eat, drink and be merry.'"

Luke 12:19

The possibility of cancer triggers a journey of tests and procedures and the tortuous wait for good news. The road starts before the diagnosis. It begins with the first signs of a potential for cancer. A high PSA test is not confirmation of cancer, but a sign that something is wrong. For others, it is a lump or a cough that won't go away. In any case, you hope the "big C" is ruled out. When it is confirmed by biopsy, you begin to hope to hear that it is not aggressive or that it was caught early. When it becomes surgery, you hope to hear they got it all and so on. For some, that good news comes quickly. For others, it comes after a long grind of tense moments and reflection. Tragically, for too many, it never comes.

It was during this journey that I learned there were notations of a high PSA (7.9) in the charts of a previous Armed Forces physical I had undergone almost two years earlier. Thankfully, my private physician, unlike the military, figured a result that high ought to be communicated to the patient. My tumor was removed in the nick of time – a full two years after that military physical.

Many who have served in the military will not be shocked by such a misfire. They can tell of similar bouts with military incompetence carrying varying degrees of consequence. Yet many of the same veterans continue to serve in spite of such tribulations. When asked why I continue to serve, I point to the one trait common to all who make a career in the military: the defective Army gene. We can't help it. It is in our blood to love the echoing sounds of cadence at sunrise, the smell of diesel, the laughs from dark humor and the warmth of camaraderie.

I rang in the new year of 2003 with my immediate family and a few friends, as I prepared for major surgery a couple of days later. In February, I resumed serving the military by assisting with the preparation of soldiers being mobilized and deployed out of Fort Dix to the Middle East for the invasion of Iraq. This was the best I could do short of volunteering for deployment again. I felt my family had been through enough, having endured the stress of two alternate futures for daddy: war or cancer.

I kept an eye on events in Afghanistan and Iraq through the media and through uniformed friends. In Iraq, I read and heard of lost initiative and opportunities squandered by U.S. leadership that valued patronage over competence. Operations designed to promote stability by meeting the needs of the population were uncoordinated and impotent, allowing the seeds of an insurgency to sprout, and then fester. U.S. resources shifted away from Afghanistan and toward Iraq. Bin Laden and his leadership fled to Pakistan, while the Taliban worked the villages in the countryside to revive violent, religious-based opposition to the NATO-backed government in Kabul.

In 2007 and 2008, it became increasingly clear we were losing the effort in Afghanistan. A growing consensus pegged Afghanistan as "the good war," the war that had to be won. Unlike Iraq, there was little doubt that the planners of the horrible 9-11 attacks, the attacks on the USS Cole and the two U.S. embassies in Kenya and Tanzania orchestrated the attacks from the pariah state of Afghanistan. Senator Barack Obama made this maxim one of the cornerstones of his campaign for the presidency in 2008 as President George W. Bush began increasing resources for the effort in Afghanistan.

By late 2009, Admiral Mullen, then Chairman of the Joint Chiefs of Staff; General David Petraeus, heroic general of the 2007 Iraq surge; and General McCrystal, then commander of all U.S. Forces in Afghanistan, and other senior leadership of the U.S. military called on now President Obama for a second surge of U.S. troops and cash for Afghanistan. There were rumors of mass resignation should he decline.[8] In December of 2009 in a speech to cadets at the U.S. Military Academy at West Point, New York, President Obama announced he was going along with his commanders' request for another surge in Afghanistan.

I was cancer free and my urge to serve was stronger than ever. That's part of the defective Army gene. Who wants to be apart from their family and the comforts of home for one year? A year without drink or sex or runny, sunny-side-up eggs? Yet we in the military seek out the chance to serve; we compete for it.

I seized an opportunity to deploy as the senior legal advisor and trainer to the Afghan National Army and the Ministry of Defense. I would have the responsibility of building a system that recruited, equipped and trained Afghan lawyers who would implement the rule of law within the

---

8 4 Threat Matrix: McChrystal to resign if not given resources for Afghanistan, Bill Roggio, Long War Journal, September 21, 2009 Available online at: http://www.longwarjournal.org/threat-matrix/archives/2009/09/mcchrystal_to_resign_if_not_gi.php; see also Secrets From Inside the Obama War Room, by Jonathon Alter, Newsweek Magazine, May 14, 2010, available online at http://www.thedailybeast.com/newsweek/2010/05/15/secrets-from-inside-the-obama-war-room.html

Afghan Army, an institution that was critical to the United States' exit strategy. I had broken a promise to myself and I was heading to the strangest of places. But I had no idea just how strange, strange could be, and I did not fully appreciate the immense personal cost. Few do.

CHAPTER 6:

READINESS

"Be dressed ready for service and keep your
lamps burning."

Luke 12:35

Preparing for a military deployment is not like preparing for a long
vacation. You must prepare the family, the body and the soul. Reservists
and guardsmen have an additional duty of preparing their employer and
co-workers.

The Army trains the soldier to be physically and tactically ready and
offers some support and guidance on preparing and supporting the family for the lonely, stress-filled months of deployment. A few decades ago,
reservists pretty much ignored the materials and briefings on activation
and deployment preparation. The only enemy we knew was Soviet Russia,
which, if angered or scared enough to wage war, would use nuclear weapons. Force deployments seemed highly unlikely.

All that changed when Iraq invaded Kuwait in 1990 and reserve units across America were activated and nearly 140,000 citizen-soldiers received the call to duty. There were limited call-ups in the 1990s, including peace-keeping missions in Bosnia and Kosovo, and the Haitian and Cuban refugee crises. The flood of call-ups opened again for reservists and guardsmen when we chose to pursue war with Iraq in 2003. Since then, with two wars on its plate and a political and budgetary mandate to keep the regular Army small, the American people have called up hundreds of thousands of reservists — many serving more than one tour of twelve to fifteen months. I say "the American people" because we are a democracy and the leaders of our nation act and derive their authority from and with the consent of the American people.

Our NATO allies provide financial compensation to employers of reservists who are called to serve, recognizing that employers suffer a financial hardship when they are compelled to fill a position with a temporary hire who will gracefully exit when Johnny or Janie come marching home again. Citizen-soldiers have to maintain delicate relationships with their employers. The law requires the employer to return soldiers to similar positions with similar pay and benefits. It also mandates a one-year period of protection against loss of employment. The employer bears the risk and cost of employing citizen-soldiers without subsidies or tax breaks. The truth is that some employers shy away from reservists for this reason.

Our reliance on part-time patriot soldiers involves financial and operational risks that start with the employer, but ultimately fall harder on the patriots, who must struggle with maintaining forward momentum and progress in his or her professional, civilian career. A part-time warrior's civilian career is essential to feeding the family for the 36 to 48 months or so that he or she is not serving on active duty. Only reservists and their families understand these consequences.

The American people, thus far, have not been willing to spend what it takes to maintain an active force big enough to handle known or likely operations, let alone a reserve force strong enough to confront the surprises that history has shown will come. I say "known" because we have waged ten years of war using reservists and guardsmen to fill the gaps. In the "Art of War," Sun Tzu advised keeping one-third of your force in reserve to meet unforeseen events. This was true in the 1970s and 1980s, when one-third of our force was Reserve and Guard. Today, it is 50% and it is used routinely to meet predictable requirements. I consider that a foolhardy tempting of fate.

At the time of my deployment, I was blessed with an employer who went above and beyond what the law requires, supplementing my salary and keeping benefits in place for my family. That security allowed me to focus my mind, body and soul on my mission and my family. Many of my comrades were not so lucky.

Research indicates deployments are hardest on adolescent girls — and I had one in 8th grade at the time I left for Afghanistan. She was acutely aware of what it meant to be a soldier serving in a war. When she was in 5th grade a classmate's sister, Army Sergeant Ashly Moyer, was serving in Iraq. My daughter's class, like many classes around our great nation, adopted Sergeant Moyer by sending her care packages and hand-made cards wishing her well. During her Rest & Relaxation (R&R) break over the Christmas holiday, Sergeant Moyer made a surprise visit to my daughter's class. Ecstatic, the school leadership called the entire school to the auditorium where the young soldier stood proud and spoke inspiringly to the young children.

A few months later, she was killed by an improvised explosive device. The school faculty somberly explained the tragic news to the students of Shohola Elementary School - a lesson that was not on any teacher's sylla-bus in this rural wooded community.

After that, my daughter would stop what she was doing and lis-ten intently when stories of U.S. casualties were reported from Iraq and Afghanistan. Sometimes she would ask me why we were there. She always took comfort that her dad was "too old to fight a war." The safety of that notion was shattered in January 2010 at the dinner table when my wife and

I told her of my pending deployment. As tears fell down her cheeks, I tried to comfort her by explaining that I would be stationed in the Green Zone near the Presidential Palace and U.S. Embassy.

Those moments of pain for my daughter would become a key reference point in my training mission as an advisor and mentor to Afghan military officers. The following day, as I arrived home from work, CBS News led its broadcast with a story about a brash attack in the Green Zone on the Presidential Palace and other ministries. I grabbed the remote and changed the channel. My wife came down the stairs asking, "What was that?" "Nothing" was all I could say.

Walking through the airport to report for duty.

Waiting with my daughter Julia for the plane

CHAPTER 7:
A MAN NEEDS A DOG

"The storyteller makes no choice, soon you will not hear
his voice, his job is to shed light, not to master."

Robert Hunter

Heading to the Ministry of Defense for the first time on foot, you notice that everywhere men are armed to the teeth, wearing uniforms that vary among the Afghan Army, Police, National Directorate of Security (NDS) intelligence service, Presidential Guard, contractors and NATO forces. The streets and sidewalks are dirty, tired and uneven, with the absolute minimum of maintenance. In the morning sun, Afghan groundskeepers are watering the streets, walkways and dirt grounds in a futile effort to keep the dust down. The bright Kabul sun reverses the effort, taking away the precious water in a matter of minutes, but the Afghan men will do it again the next day. At the gate to the Ministry of Defense, the Afghan Guards direct NATO forces who enter to empty their weapons. Suffice it to say that I and others long in the tooth in the service of the U.S. and other NATO countries felt most unsafe when around armed, uniformed

Afghans. Some fellow advisors who wore the crossed arrows of Special Forces would reload once beyond the gate and I was not going to argue with their wisdom.

Inside the Ministry of Defense, the beauty of the rose gardens against the background of the snowcapped mountains makes you forget for a second that you are in one of the most violent lands man has ever known. One of my Afghan General advisees, Major General Amon Nooristani, with the help of my interpreters, once walked me through these gardens after a feast of sheep, chicken and several different rice dishes, telling the story of the battles for Kabul in 2001. From one mountain top, the Uzbek warlord Dostom pounded the city, while the Hazaras dominated what is now known as "TV hill" because of all the antennas on it. Opposite these mountains sat Massoud's forces across the river. Within the compound, the Pashtun Taliban had let the gardens become overgrown and overrun by nasty wild dogs.

Today, however, the gardens were manicured, and the dogs resembled Old Yeller, well fed from the cafeteria scraps provided by Afghan soldiers and NATO soldiers alike, especially one Canadian Colonel, Brock Millman. Major General Nooristani, the chief of the Ministry of Defense Legal, and Brigadier General Karim, the top uniformed lawyer, were about to meet me, the latest in a long line of American advisors, inexperienced in the ways of the Afghans.

Inside the headquarters building with no elevators (elevators require maintenance, which is anathema to the Afghans), getting to the fifth floor is a workout, stepping over the bird droppings as you make your way past Afghan men, some in suits, others in uniform and others in traditional loose-fitting wraps, with long gray beards and turbans. By the time you get to the top of the steps, your heart pounds as your lungs struggle to make good use of the foul-smelling, polluted air, which is thin to boot at 6,000 feet. A four-foot-tall elderly man with few teeth jumps up from his chair with a smile to greet the westerners: "Salaam Alaikum!" There are several men sitting around the hall, all day, every day, as there are on every floor. Waiting in the general's office suite are several more men, young, able-bodied officers of the Afghan National Army. Their only job is to sit in the waiting area to greet callers and to be ready to fetch files and deliver messages whenever the general beckons using his wireless door chime. Visitors seeking favors that range from jobs to resolving legal issues, also wait in the anteroom.

Meetings with Afghans are typified by a lack of agenda, disruptions by cell phones, televisions that seem to run 24 hours a day, tea, of course, and depending on the Afghan's stature, snacks ranging from simple candy to elaborate spreads of nuts, raisins, figs, cookies and cakes. Cigarette smoke is common. Some hosts chain smoke like there is no tomorrow, a typical Afghan sentiment. Guests are wise to enter cautiously and respectfully, allowing the Afghans to adjust the seating order to match the rank of the hosts and guests in an unrehearsed but no doubt precise manner. If already seated in the position of honor when an Afghan of unknown stature enters, one should rise to greet the caller and gesture to your seat. The Afghans will make sure the new arrival will find the right seat and, if it is yours, so be it and take note of this man of import. The first round of tea and snacks are obligatory, to be enjoyed and appreciated as a gauge of successful rapport. If more tea and snacks arrive without asking, it is a sign of success. If lunch appears, the rapport is robust. If you are asked whether you would like another cup of tea or to stay for lunch, you have been politely told your welcome has been worn out.

As an advisor to the Afghans, my first meetings were marked by introductions that included questions about family and origin. Photographs are also part of the drill, with the Afghans stoic in their poses, reminiscent of the vintage photos of Native Americans. The Afghans learned that my birth village was a place called the Bronx and that while my father was born in the same village, in the same hospital and delivered by the same doctor as me, my mother was from an altogether different country, Argentina. Some generals are reserved, a trait that applies to most Afghans. Others can seem downright bombastic, with tall and long tales that can go on for what seems like hours. Within those winded, seemingly pointless diatribes against people, places and things are important cues — some subtle, some blunt — that need to be noted mentally as part of the bigger picture.

Ministry of Defense positions are filled with active generals who wear civilian suits as part of a lame effort to demonstrate a sense of civilian control of the military — a concept near and dear to the U.S. and its NATO allies. The structure of Western aid, however, compounds the Afghan cultural incentive to retain military rank. One such officer was the Ministry of Defense Inspector General, a civilian position occupied by a two-star Major General of Hazaran ethnicity. In what I learned has become a ritual with all new advisors brought to his office, the general explained the pressures of the job. The Ministry of Defense provides him with an armored SUV (paid for by the U.S. taxpayers, of course) and fuel for official business. How can he not use the car to deliver his children to and from school when there are enemies looking to do him harm, he asked. Proudly, he showed gunshot wounds to his legs and stomach. He called in his driver, who proceeded to take off his shirt with his one good arm, sporting horrific scars all over his torso. The driver, the general explained, was mistaken for him during the attack. So now, the general takes care of the driver by giving him a job at the Ministry of Defense. It was the thought of these incidents that led me to politely decline the general's invitation to his home for a meal.

Major General Nooristani, another civilian-suited general, was the chief of the Ministry of Defense Legal Department. Lacking in formal legal education, he was otherwise educated as a professionally trained artillery officer and had spent time in Russian and Indian military institutions. Like many Afghans, his last name is derived from his place of origin, in this case, the province of Nuristan. Nuristan had been known as Kafiristan, the land of Kafirs or non-believers, until it succumbed to Islam in the late 1800s.

An animated, sometimes unruly chain smoker, he too had an almost scripted presentation for western guests that might have some influence over the U.S. largesse that drives virtually all economic activity in Afghanistan. The boiled down version of his 60-minute presentation script was a critique of the wealth accumulated by corrupt Afghan National Police prosecutors and judges, all of whom he claimed to be three and four-star generals. To counter this evil, the general insisted, the legal personnel inside the Ministry of Defense and Afghan National Army must be promoted, lest they too become corrupt out of economic necessity. A point of reference is appropriate here: the average Afghan household income in 2009 was $420 per year. Thanks to the support of U.S. taxpayers, the pay of a two-star Afghan general was then $1,200 per month – more than 300 times that of a true civilian.

Prior to my first visit to the Ministry of Defense, the State Department sent a message to advisors noting that President Karzai had just appointed a new governor in one of the northern provinces who was a former commander of forces against the Russians and a sarenwol, which is Dari for prosecutor. The message asked advisors to take note if their advisees had anything to say about this new governor. In the parlance of the advisory group, the State Department was asking the military advisors for "atmospherics" or what Winston Churchill described as measuring the mood.

Asked about this man, Major General Nooristani began to tell a story that would have been long enough had I spoken and understood Dari, but through translation, went on in ways that can't be captured in writing.

With steady intensity, he told me this parable.

A man's dog has died. This man was sad as he searched near and far for a new companion, but he could not find one that could live up to the memories of his lost friend. One day, he came across a dog that had a handsome face. The dog stood proud and alert. The owner came out from his shop to meet the man looking over his canine. "You have noticed my dog," the shop owner said. "He is a fine animal and he is well educated." "What do you mean?" asked the man who had lost his dog. "He speaks many languages — English, Dari, Pashto and Arabic," boasted the owner. "You are not a serious man," replied the man. "You insult me with these claims."

The shop owner calmed the man and said, "No sir. Do not take offense. You need only ask the dog yourself, he will tell you all about himself."

The man looked disbelievingly at the owner, and then turned to the dog. "You speak Dari?" "Balle," replied the dog, answering "yes" in Dari. The man was stunned.

The general continued telling the tale, exhaling smoke through his nose.

"Tell me more about yourself," the man demanded of the dog.

"I speak many languages, and I am a trained police dog. I am so good that I am the dog that found Saddam Hussein." The man was impressed and told the shop owner that he must have this dog, asking for his price.

"You may have this dog for free," replied the owner.

"Free? That makes no sense," the man said. "This dog is educated; he is a trained police dog; he captured Saddam Hussein! How can he be free?"

The general put out his cigarette, leaned forward, and delivered the punch line with deep, dramatic conviction: "Because this dog is a liar!"

The general's expression turned to anger; his nostrils flared as he screamed at his western guests while pounding his fist on the table: "And this dog is worth MORE than the new governor! He is not a lawyer! He was never a commander! He has no education!"

It was almost as if Nooristani had read the State Department's message.

MOD DOGS

The Ministry of Defense Grounds

Afghan National Army Legal Officers

The Ministry of Defense Legal Chief and Staff

CHAPTER 8:
A MAN NEEDS A WIFE

"Go West Young Man!"

Attributed to Horace Greeley

There is much that is strange to the Westerner who visits this land-locked country where the year is 1389; The laws of Islam reign supreme by virtue of its constitution; More than 70% of the population can't read their native language, let alone Arabic, which forms the only official version of the Koran; and attacks using gas on girls' schools are common. There is still a substantial population of men that don't like the idea of girls going to school. These men release cooking gas or propane into these schools to shut them down and scare the parents from sending the girls to school. To the enlightened, these observations may seem crass and culturally insensitive. However, there is one constituency that seems to vote in a way that affirms much that is wrong with Afghanistan - the educated youth.

Afghan young people vote with their feet, by seizing any opportunity to flee Afghanistan never to return. In June of 2011, the Department of State quietly ended a student exchange program for Afghan children because of the numbers violating the terms of their VISAs by fleeing to Canada.[9] A young, college-educated Afghan woman who was consistently courteous, diligent and stoic in the face of local men who taunted her with chants of "whore," spoke of her hatred of Afghanistan and how she is doing everything she can to leave. Her solution for bringing hope to Afghanistan is to eliminate every Afghan male over the age of eighteen. Calling her sentiments harsh is certainly an understatement, but they are telling nonetheless of the seemingly intractable problems that curse Afghanistan and keep it from being anything but Afghanistan.

Many young, uneducated, politically unconnected Afghans flee the Afghan National Army after suffering the indignations of man rape, being fed food better left for rodents or finding themselves continuously in the harsh combat environment of the south, while others roam in the relative safety of the halls of the Ministry of Defense or other Kabul-based units. Commonly referred to as AWOL, that stands for absent without leave, the issue was the subject of my first tasking from Major General Hogg, then Deputy Commanding General for Army. A soldier's general, Major General Hogg would stand in line with others to get his chow, taking the opportunity to talk to soldiers, sailors, airmen and marines who might be around him. He would venture to the Morale Welfare Recreation (MWR) area outside the Green Bean Coffee Shop to join soldiers smoking or enjoying coffee after hours — the only two vices allowed by General Order Number One. There were other general officers who acted as Major General Hogg did, and there were others who deemed their time too important to stand in line. They would direct their aides to fetch their supper.

While still suffering from severe jet lag from my journey, I found myself in a meeting with the Command Inspector General, who also served as the advisor to the Afghan Inspectors General and the advisor

9 Exchange program cancelled after Afghan students flee U.S. for Canada, TheStar.com, June 13, 2011

to the Afghan Assistant Minister of Defense for Personnel and Education. Our discussion focused on solutions to the Afghan AWOL problem. The word "problem," I learned, was one of many words that were in disfavor by the Command. "Challenge" was viewed as less negative. Also, the Command preferred to speak of the challenge of "attrition," instead of AWOL. Attrition — the rate at which personnel leave by choice or due to death, illness, or termination — is a challenge common to all organizations.

The Coalition's officially reported Afghan attrition rate of 2%, as of late 2010, does not sound so bad until you realize that the rate is monthly and equates to losing 24% of your force in a year. The attrition rate does not capture the Afghans who leave for long periods of time, then return to the rolls with no consequence because of Presidential Amnesty decrees that are issued with the certainty of the Earth's orbit. It also does not account for the Afghan ghost soldiers - ghosts not in the tradition of U.S. Intelligence and Special Operations players — but in the tradition of crooked unions who create "no show" jobs for special friends. From my battlefield circulation around Afghanistan with my advisee, it was clear that the reported rates of AWOL, as high as 29% in a Corps that was thought to have the best retention rate, were actually much higher. A more meaningful metric would be "truly present for duty."

AWOL soldiers of the Afghan National Army fall into five categories.

1. There are opportunists who wish to serve only where there is money to be made, such as doctors who joined to draw salary from the Afghan National Army while devoting most of their time to private practice in Kabul. These doctors simply refuse to report when they learn they are being assigned to Kandahar or Helmand, where fighting is severe, and the need is greatest.

2. There are infiltrators who join with the intent to get training, equipment, and information about the ways of the Afghan National Army, only so that they can be better prepared to attack

the Afghan National Army or Coalition troops after they desert to join their brothers and cousins in the Taliban.

3. There are "copers" who join at the urging of their village elders or to make a living but who eventually flee abysmal living conditions or continuous service in heavy combat areas or who view the Army as a seasonal job to be abandoned when the growing season arrives.

4. There are the intimidated who flee in response to the infamous night letters from the Taliban threatening to harm the families of those who support the government.

5. There are those who abandon their country altogether by deserting when they are sent to the U.S. or other countries for training.

The initial solution of the Western soldier to the AWOL problem is obvious: discipline, not amnesty. But the target of the discipline is not so obvious. Use of a wide disciplinary net against all who go AWOL would be a grave mistake. The forces of the Kabul-based government are considered by many in Afghan villages to be as foreign as Coalition troops. Imagine those troops coming to arrest young Mohammed, who fled the Army and returned to his family with tales of horrible food, chilled nights without blankets, beatings at the hands of officers and Non Commissioned Officers, sickness without medicine, and tales of alcohol and drug use among his commanders. You do not need to be an expert in counter-insurgency to know who the village will support.

There are, of course, deserters worthy of punishment: the doctors and other officers who refuse to report to their place of duty in combat zones, the doctors and nurses who abandon their post daily in Kabul to make money at their private clinics, and the military judge from 205th Corps who walked away from his service obligation to get a better position with the Supreme Court, a government institution that could not care less about the service obligation of the officer.

When asked about a solution to the AWOL problems, leaders of the Afghan National Army Legal Corps were unequivocal in their response - eliminate the abysmal leaders of the Ministry of Defense and Afghan National Army who are more concerned with tribal politics and enriching themselves than with taking care of soldiers. One senior U.S. general officer commented that if he were king for a day, he would eliminate 75% of the officer corps of the Afghan National Army — a seeming validation of Afghan National Army Legal's solution. That same general made it clear he was not king for a day and was resigned to a conclusion that these officers were and will remain in charge.

To unravel why the U.S. and its Coalition allies are making only "measured fragile and reversible progress" in building the Afghan National Army, you need to understand the prime directive of the Afghan National Army. Its driving mission is to provide Afghans with jobs, prestige, and wealth accumulation opportunities on an ethnically balanced basis.

Contrast this to what U.S. Army cadets were taught in the last century: the mission of the U.S. Army was to fight and win the nation's wars. If the Army could accomplish the tasks essential to fighting and winning the nation's wars, it could adjust to do many other things it was called upon to do. More recently, toward the end of the W. Bush presidency, the Army was given a second tenet: to carry out stability operations with equal ability to that of conducting combat operations. The wisdom of this additional costly tenet is worthy of volumes of scholarly treatises not attempted here, although this story should give you an idea of the unintended consequences.

To those who serve at the Afghan ministerial level for more than a few months, the frustrating difference between the two forces is strikingly apparent. To most of the Afghan National Army leadership, their soldiers are profit centers — an opportunity to extract money from their salaries, their food, and the shelter and clothing allotments within the unit budget. Higher level commands have additional income opportunities from shaking down contractors who are in the business of providing goods and services to the Afghan National Army, including contractors hired by the U.S. to build facilities for the Afghan troops.

This shamelessness, or what many senior U.S. commanders would downplay as a "cultural framework," extends to medical care for its own troops. The Afghan National Army leadership is either unwilling or unable to see to it that medical resources (paid for and provided by the U.S.) are delivered at no cost to the Afghan National Army soldier and his family as we intended. To understand this reality is to understand the AWOL problem.

At one point in the Coalition's effort to encourage accountability at the leadership level, we were tasked to define the length of service obligations for soldiers, officers and noncommissioned officers under Afghan law. The answer to the question of how long Afghan soldiers were required to serve depended on whom you asked, an interpretive subjectivity that is commonplace in Afghanistan. Definitive law libraries are non-existent. Laws are written in Dari and Pashto, both official Afghan languages, but each one translates to English differently. For enlisted soldiers and non-commissioned officers there was little dispute about the required length of service, but for officers the answers ranged from zero, to ten, to twenty years.

Around this time, *Rolling Stone* magazine published an article that created a crisis in wartime military leadership unseen since the famous public dispute between General Douglas MacArthur and President Harry S. Truman during the Korean War. General Stan McCrystal and his staff had been held up in France by the same volcano that had delayed my group's deployment into theater. This gave them additional face time with the "Rolling Stone" reporter, whose published account of their pub time and disparaging comments toward the Obama administration brought an early retirement to the Commander of ISAF (COMISAF).

Within hours after General Petraeus left President Obama's side at the press conference announcing his new command of all U.S. and NATO Forces in Afghanistan, he sent a message to his soon to be direct subordinate, Lieutenant General Caldwell, Commander of the NATO Training Mission in Afghanistan. Petraeus stated that one of his top two priorities upon taking command would be to implement a clearly defined Afghan military service obligation.

The issue was sensitive because of media attention in the U.S. to the problem of Afghan officers who were deserting while in the U.S. for schooling. Word of this Petraeus message came to me as I was standing by to brief service obligations with Brigadier General Gary Patton and Dr. Kem, civilian deputy to Lieutenant General Caldwell. A Lieutenant Colonel advisor to the Afghan Ministry of Defense section responsible for training and personnel had been tapped to take the lead for this task and I was ordered to provide him support. The deadline given was August 1, 2010, just under six weeks away. This seemed impossible, but, as Major General Nooristani would say, "This is Afghanistan, where the impossible is easy and the easy is impossible."

Tackling the service obligation issue required tackling the issue of deserting Afghan officers in the U.S. and other countries. As a practical matter, assuming there was a service obligation at all, what could be done to prevent an Afghan who is willing to abandon his homeland from abandoning service to his homeland?

The Afghans had a mechanism in place called the "guarantor." A guarantor was a person of stature who signed a document vouching for the character of the candidate for a commission as an officer or an assignment out of country. The guarantor also promised to pay the costs of his training and equipment should he fail to serve or return as promised. As a member of a niche practice of law in the U.S. known as suretyship, this concept was well known to me. The Afghans required that candidates for officer slots and Out of Country Training (OCT) find someone to post a bond in their behalf similar to a bail bond, where a family member or friend promises to forfeit money or collateral should the accused fail to return for his or her day in court.

Enforcing the current guarantor system seemed like the logical solution to the OCT desertion problem. But, in discussions with the legal departments and the personnel departments of the Ministry of Defense, we learned that these guaranties were never meant to be anything more than character references. The economic aspect as written was unenforceable under Islamic law, because the guarantors were poor people who could never pay. An unconscionable agreement that the law refuses to enforce is a concept known to every Western lawyer.

A closer look at this Afghan guaranty, or what we in the surety industry would call a surety bond, was warranted and I started adding language that might make it more effective in preventing OCT desertion. One afternoon, while dining with a member of the Afghan National Army's judiciary who had once been a justice with the Afghan Supreme Court, the topic of debt collection came up. The judge explained that a debtor who refused to pay a debt that he could afford to pay could be detained until he made good on his debt. A debtor who could not pay would be released to his village with a requirement that he return to the court on a monthly basis to make a payment of some amount, even a pint of goat's milk or an egg, to show good faith to the court and the creditor. These concepts sounded familiar to one who has dealt with the U.S. Bankruptcy Courts.

When the judge learned that I was struggling to come up with an enforceable guaranty, he smiled and said he had recently issued an opinion to the Ministry of Defense on the enforceability of a guaranty in a case involving a general officer guarantor and his nephew who had deserted. When asked of his position, he said they absolutely were enforceable and he recommended that the Ministry of Defense hold back some of the general's pay. The Ministry did not like his opinion because many of the guarantors of the deserted OCT officers were generals and colonels — not peasants as senior members of the Ministry of Defense had claimed. The judge supported enforcement because he felt it would motivate people to stop signing guarantees on behalf of "stupid" people.

Armed with this revelation, the advisory team began pushing the Ministry of Defense from all sides to get a strict OCT policy in place and to enforce existing guarantees. The discussions between the Western advisors and the Afghans were heated and long-winded, seemingly going nowhere.

At one point, Major General Nooristani commented that many of the students in the U.S. getting military education have no military status, an odd comment which I reported to the Security Assistance Office (SAO) that is responsible for military training of Afghan personnel within the United States. The SAO replied cocksure that here was no merit to Nooristani's comment because only members of the Afghan military were sent to the U.S. for military schooling.

One Afghan general officer from the Ministry's Personnel and Education section pulled his U.S. Advisor aside to tell him the true nature of the problem. He acknowledged that the guarantees were enforceable and that many of the guarantors were, in fact, senior leaders of the Ministry of Defense and Afghan National Army. However, he went on, the true problem lay in the unintended consequences of enforcing the guarantees. If the Coalition insisted on enforcement, he said, many of these officers will leave the Ministry of Defense and Afghan National Army to join forces with the Taliban.

Many of us actually felt that this would be a good thing and imagined the Coalition providing air assets to deliver these "heroes" of Afghanistan directly to the Taliban lines.

The service obligation challenge took an unexpected twist in late June 2011, thanks to action by the Afghan Parliament. Fed up with Karzai's disrespect toward Parliament's constitutional role in governance, such as his refusal to subject Supreme Court Justices or Ministry heads to Parliamentary approval, the Parliament passed five laws by a veto-proof, two-thirds majority. The largely illiterate body likely had little idea of the content or import of the laws being passed; they knew only that Karzai had opposed their passage and that was good enough reason to overwhelmingly vote them into law as a last act of defiance before going into permanent recess for the general Parliamentary elections scheduled for September. One of these laws was called the "Inherent Law for Officers and Non-Commissioned Officers," aka ILON (pronounced eye-lon). While it contained some short-comings, the law was extremely helpful on the Active-Duty Service Obligation issue because it provided the legal basis for a 10-year commitment for officers.

In the greater scheme of things, ILON was the by-product of a promising development: the emergence of the Parliament as a second center of gravity within the Government of the Islamic Republic of Afghanistan to act as a democratic check on the power of Karzai's presidency. Later in my tour, when the Command tasked me with the additional duty of serving as chief of the Ministry of Defense's Parliamentary Advisory Team, these hopes would be dashed by Karzai's continued systematic marginalization of Parliament. But for now, we ran hard with the new law to deliver on Petraeus' priority goal. We believed Parliament had definitively settled the question using power granted to them by the Afghan constitution.

But alas, this was Afghanistan. As part of the law-making process, the Taqneen – a division of the Ministry of Justice — reduces to writing any proposed legislation, whether originating with Parliament or the Executive branch. The Taqneen places the following clause in every draft law: "This law shall become effective upon publication in the Official Gazette." The Gazette is operated by the Taqneen, which is part of the Ministry of Justice, which is controlled by Karzai. The Afghans in the Ministry of Defense Legal and Personnel & Education were quick to point out that ILON was not law until the Taqneen published it – and the Taqneen were in no hurry. Energized by Petraeus' new command, determined to meet his objective and convinced that we were again being played for fools by the Afghan Ministry of Defense leadership, I sought second, third and fourth opinions.

Across Kabul, the "Dean of Faculty Law" of Kabul University was adamant that the Constitution was clear and unambiguous on this point. ILON became a primary law of Afghanistan when it was approved by two thirds of the Wolesi Jirga, the lower house of Parliament. Publication, while a practical necessity to let the people know of the law, was not a part of the law-making process. The First Deputy Minister of Defense Naziri, a trained lawyer and former chief prosecutor, concurred with the dean. To seal an authoritative interpretation, we planned to meet the head of the Taqneen, Mr. Halim, arguably the most influential lawyer in Afghanistan.

Mr. Halim was known to have a sweet tooth, so we made sure to bring a box of Girl Scout cookies, courtesy of one of many friends back home. Needing transportation for the legal and personnel team making the call on Mr. Halim, we turned to Sergeant Major Joseph Pedroza, who was an advisor to the Afghan Sergeant Major of the Army and a multi-combat tour All American of the famed 82nd Airborne Division. Pedroza brought his two-vehicle movement outside of Camp Eggers to meet my team. Dressed in full battle rattle that included his combat goggles, the Sergeant Major thoroughly briefed us on the vehicles, communications and available weaponry, pointing to his machine gun, the hundreds of extra rounds in the center compartment, his pistols and the extra magazines in the glove compartment, two fragmentation grenades on his ammo belt and a bag of grenades under the passenger seat. I acknowledged the briefing points and told him I was packing a pistol, two magazines of fifteen rounds each, an iPod and a box of Girl Scout cookies. He smiled and we proceeded to the Taqneen.

Upon arrival, the Afghan National Army guards refused entry to those bearing arms, demanding that they be surrendered as a condition of entry. My response was the same given to security at the InterContinental Hotel who made a similar demand: *hell no*. There was no way uniformed soldiers were going anywhere outside of a Coalition base without a weapon. The civilian-clothed members of our team went in to what was a successful meeting while those of us in uniform stayed with the Sergeant Major's bag of hand grenades. Halim confirmed that ILON was law despite the publication issue. Portions of the law unrelated to Active Duty Service Obligation would be fixed by a compromise being worked out between

Parliament and Karzai, but for our concerns, ILON was law and the basis for the comprehensive Active Duty Service Obligation policy confirmed.

Having navigated the obfuscation thrown our way by the Afghan Ministry of Defense leadership, the Active Duty Service Obligation policy finally got traction. The Minister of Defense executed the policy on August 8, 2010 — seven days beyond the impossible deadline but only a day after the Minister returned from a week-long trip out of country. But it wasn't long before a new challenge emerged that would provide an embarrassing example of good intentions gone awry.

A young Afghan male — "Cadet K" — was about to graduate from a U.S. military academy with no military status in the Afghan Army and no intention of returning to Afghanistan to make good on the $400,000 investment in his education by U.S. taxpayers. He was engaged to be married to an Afghan American woman and, thus, would be eligible for resident alien status.

American families must secure the nomination of their U.S. Senator or House Representative before a son or daughter could even be considered for admission to these highly sought-after schools. But the files of the Security Assistance Office contained very little explanation of how Cadet K had been selected to come to the U.S. for a free education. What was clear from SAO's files and from what the Afghans were saying was that the Afghans didn't want Cadet K selected then and they didn't want him in their military now. No one at Camp Eggers knew who selected Cadet K or why, or at least no one would admit knowing. Perhaps the Afghans preferred to send someone based on nepotism, or someone willing to pay the appropriate fee for such a plum assignment. Anything coveted in the Ministry of Defense would typically be given to the family member of a Ministry official or to the highest bidder. Cadet K was an interpreter with solid English skills needed for Out-of-Country Training in the U.S., but he appeared unconnected to the Afghan leadership.

Lieutenant General Caldwell had a potential public relations disaster on his hands. With many Americans' college funds suffering in a bad economy, no one would want to hear that the U.S. was stupidly giving away college educations to Afghans who won't serve their country. He pulled out all of the stops to arrange for a service obligation on the part of Cadet K within the Afghan National Army. Seeking leverage to induce Cadet K into a service contract with the Afghan National Army, messages were sent to the Secretary of Defense seeking to block the cadet's graduation and another sent to the Secretary of State seeking to block his resident alien application. Neither seemed willing to intervene. In the meantime, negotiations with the cadet began. A 10-year commitment was out of the question for this cadet, but something significantly less seemed possible. Five years was proposed, and the Minister of Defense indicated to NATO Training Mission - Afghanistan leadership that this would be acceptable.

An agreement was drafted and presented to the Ministry of Defense Legal for review. Major General Nooristani gave it the thumbs down, pointing out that the agreement was illegal under ILON. The active duty service obligation for an officer was a minimum of 10 years. To give this cadet only a five-year obligation was illegal. The general officer of the branch who was to sign the agreement with Cadet K refused to do so. He spoke with Major General Nooristani on the phone while I was present. My interpreter could hear the other end of the conversation and kept me apprised of the tenor. The general refused to take part in signing an agreement that was "clearly corrupt." The general officer speaking to Nooristani was considered by the Coalition to be amongst the most corrupt officials in a government ranked as the world's most corrupt, second only to Somalia which has no military. Major General Nooristani concurred with the general's assessment that the arrangement would be "corrupt." If Cadet K got a free education in the U.S. and then he gets a shorter service obligation, how would that look to the other young Afghan officers?

I explained that this was very important to Lieutenant General Caldwell and that the Ministry of Defense had no greater friend than he. I urged him to convince the general or even the Minister to sign the five-year contract with Cadet K. Major General Nooristani then began to tell me a story through my interpreter, a young Pashtun lawyer. Also present was an elderly two-star Afghan general who was going to be the new chief of staff of Ground Forces Command.

Nooristani began. In Afghanistan, marriages are arranged by the parents. Sometimes the parents of the groom trick their son by showing him a picture of a pretty girl, but then on the day of the wedding, an ugly bride appears at the ceremony. A young man approached his father and said, "Father, it is time for me to have a wife." The father agreed to arrange it. The son warned his father that the bride must be beautiful; that he would not fall for the trick of a fake picture. The father, taken aback, looked over his son, then said, "OK son, but you must do your part to help us get you a pretty wife." "What must I do?" asked the son.

At this point in the translation, the Ground Forces general literally fell out of his chair onto the floor laughing. My interpreter, who had a dark complexion, blushed and shook his head. With a nervous grin, he said to me "Sir, I cannot translate this story anymore." Nooristani grimaced at him, shook his hand at him and ordered him to proceed while the other general slowly picked himself up from the floor, still laughing.

I asked the interpreter to please proceed, and he did so.

The father said to the son, "If you have a big penis, it will help us get you a pretty wife, but your mother and I know that you do not have a big penis. So, you must make it bigger by pulling it and stretching it every day."

"How long must I make it?" asked the son.

"So long that you can even fuck yourself," the father replied…"Once you have it that long, come back to me and I will know you are ready for your beautiful wife."

The son worked on his penis every day, pulling and stretching it. Then one day he went to his father and said, "OK, father, I finally have my penis so long that I can even fuck myself."

The father replied, "Good, then you no longer need me to find you a wife because you can fuck yourself!"

With that, Nooristani looked sternly at me., "That is the conversation Cadet K is having with Lieutenant General Caldwell!"

Of course, I knew better. The story was symbolic of a conversation — but not between an Afghan boy and an American general. It was a parable that described the relationship between the Afghan leadership and the U.S. leadership.

In the end, Cadet K got his diploma, presumably got his resident alien status, and never served a single day on behalf of the U.S. or Afghanistan military, despite our investment in his education. The ILON law had not been published in the Taqneen when I departed Afghanistan in March 2011. That summer, President Karzai again issued an amnesty for all soldiers and officers who had gone AWOL.

So much for the "challenge" of service obligations.

General Petraeus arrives on Camp Eggers on July 4, 2010, the day he assumed command of all U.S. and NATO Forces in Afghanistan.

Lieutenant General Caldwell presenting a mid-tour award to Lieutenant Colonel Mike Tayman and me for the implementation of an Afghan Active-Duty Service Obligation.

CHAPTER 9:

IT'S A BUZKASHI! THE AFGHAN'S LOVE-HATE RELATIONSHIP WITH CHAOS

"God will stretch out over Edom the measuring line of
chaos and the plumb line of desolation."

Isaiah 34:11

The calf is beheaded. Then its hoofs are removed to spare the rough
hands of the hundred or so horsemen. The calf's body is dropped into the
center of the field and soon the horsemen are scrambling in a formation
similar to a rugby scrum. A horseman grabs the carcass only to have it
snatched by another. That man's mount is pushed and bitten by another
horse, while yet another horseman emerges from the scrum with the prize.
Part of the crowd cheers on, believing a score has taken place by their
favored stallion. But then another grabs the calf and the referee declares
this grab to be the scoring event.

Quickly, the crowd aligns itself with the warlords whose horsemen
lie in opposite positions on this outrageous call. It's like any sporting event

where the referee makes a controversial call, except here the audience is very political and you can see how they take sides in the argument.

The Tooi-wala, the Khan who has sponsored this grand game and all of the festivities surrounding it, looks on with unease at the chaos that begins to unfold on the field. His referee is unable to maintain control of the situation. All who have come to this grand event are snidely taking note of the Tooi-wala's demonstrated weakness. Then, a neighboring Khan who is aligned with rivals to the Tooi-wala's network, or qaum, steps in to mediate the situation. He succeeds, preventing one side from walking out on the tournament and allowing both sides of the dispute, which includes vast numbers of the crowd from different qaums, to save face. Chaos is averted, and the Tooi-wala, outwardly grateful to the peacemaking Khan, is humiliated that someone outside his qaum had to make peace. The Tooi-wala lost control and was forced to rely on a rival to restore order. The tournament could not have turned out worse, except for maybe all-out war. Then again, the Tooi-wala thinks, maybe war would have been better than to have ceded prestige to the neighboring Khan.

Such is sport and politics in Afghanistan.

Coming to understand Afghan culture can be an ordeal. Winston Churchill, who accompanied British forces into Afghanistan in the late 1800s, described the challenge:

> So extraordinary is the inversion of ideas and motives among Afghans that it may be said that those who know them best, know them least, and the more logical the mind of the student the less he is able to understand of the subject.[10]

> The difficult language and peculiar characters of the tribesmen are the study of a lifetime. A knowledge of the local conditions, of the power and influence of the khans (warlords), or other rulers of the people; of the general history and traditions of the country, is a task which must be entirely specialized . .

10 Malakand Field Force, page 18

. I do not believe that such are to be found in the army. The military profession is alone sufficient to engross the attention of the most able and accomplished man.[11]

General McCrystal, on the 10th anniversary of the U.S. invasion of Afghanistan, stated that the U.S. has operated with an overly simplistic view of Afghan history and culture. "Most of us, me included, had a very superficial understanding of the situation and history, and we had a frighteningly simplistic view of recent history, the last 50 years," he said.[12]

The U.S. Army had done little to effectively prepare officers assigned to be advisors to the Afghans. There are some canned presentations on Afghan tribalism and culture, but little else until arrival in country. At NATO Training Mission - Afghanistan, there was a day and a half course, which recently has been expanded to one week. In an effort to overcome the U.S. cultural deficiency, General McCrystal advocated a program called "AfPak Hands" before the President replaced him in June 2010.

The AfPak Hands program selects officers who are willing to undergo months of cultural and linguistic training on Afghanistan and Pakistan. The Hands commit to multiple tours to the region and to continue training while home between deployments. Every soldier, sailor, marine and airman trains between deployments. What is different with the AfPak Hands program is that the training and work continues to be focused solely on Afghanistan and Pakistan, while others rotate to new units that have a focus on other regions of the world.

General McCrystal's intent for this program was to have AfPak Hands members live and work among the Afghans to foster better understanding between the peoples of the region and to develop mutual trust, which would help the U.S. and its Coalition partners strengthen the Afghan Security Forces and legitimize the Afghan government.

---

11 Ibid. Page 98.

12 U.S. had 'frighteningly simplistic' view of Afghanistan, says McChrystal, Declan Walsh in Islamabad, guardian.co.uk, the Guardian, Friday 7 October 2011

The first cadre of AfPak Hands received an introductory mission briefing shortly after commencement of the program, from none other than Admiral Mike Mullin, the chairman of the Joint Chiefs of Staff.[13] Admiral Mullin told the Hands they were selected on short notice due to the urgency of need (there were no volunteers in the audience) and because they were "the best of the best of the best." He proceeded to outline a program that drew heavily on an article written by Major Jim Gant, of the U.S. Army Special Forces, entitled, "One Tribe at a Time." Gant advocated embedding a dedicated U.S. advisor into key Afghan/Pakistani villages and organizations, similar to the experience recorded by T.E. Lawrence, also known as Lawrence of Arabia. Lawrence was a British officer who, in the 1920s and 30s became an expert on the Arab people and lands.

When asked about the force protection policies in place and the latitude Hands would have to operate as intended, McCrystal stated that all the subordinate commanders in theater had already been directed to accept the higher risk that the Hands mission would require.

In spring 2010, McCrystal addressed the same group of Hands on their way to Afghanistan, declaring them to be his "300." That reference evoked the criticality of their mission, special status, and likely degree of danger. Later that spring, McCrystal again addressed these Hands and re-iterated his intent that they go out amongst the population, looking and living like Afghans. They were to shed their armor and the hunker-down-behind-the-FOB (Forward Operating Base) walls mentality that had paralyzed Coalition effectiveness in building constructive relationships with the Afghans. McCrystal spent much of his career as a shadow warrior in Special Operations and was known for his blunt language. He made it clear that he expected some of them would be captured and perhaps

---

13 The briefings of Admiral Mullen and General McCrystal have been relayed to me by a trusted colleague who was present at them.

beheaded, but he expected them to carry on with the exceptionally important mission for which they were selected. The Hands, like all military, were soldiers first.

But Mullin's and McCrystal's vision for the program was never realized at NATO Training Mission - Afghanistan, the three-star command responsible for developing, training and equipping the Afghan Security Forces. One senior command official at NATO Training Mission - Afghanistan told me that the AfPak Hands program was a useless waste of time. While NATO Training Mission - Afghanistan had a number of Hands assigned, not one was allowed the leeway intended by McCrystal regarding movements among the Afghans. NATO Training Mission - Afghanistan leadership was risk averse to the point of disregarding COMISAF's intent, appearing less concerned for the potential benefits from AfPak Hand engagement with Afghans than the potential distractions and fallout to commanders' reputations and careers that might come from the publicity and investigation into the death of a Hand.

One glaring example of risk aversion and frustrated commander's intent involved a member of my Parliamentary Affairs team. I wanted her go to Parliament to establish relationships with members as a way of developing the second leg of the three-legged stool of government: Executive; Judiciary; and Legislative. To go into Parliament would require civilian clothes, traditional scarf to cover the head and no weapon. NATO Training Mission - Afghanistan made it clear they would not approve of such activity.

After General Petraeus took command on July 4, 2010, he reaffirmed that he was on the same page with McCrystal when it came to AfPak Hands. A senior leader from the Army Development team asked General Petraeus if my subordinate, a member of the Legal and Parliamentary Affairs team, ought to be allowed to go to Parliament in civilian clothes without a weapon. Petraeus mentioned her by name in his response and agreed she should be allowed to go to Parliament without a weapon in civilian clothes. There was no ambiguity in his answer.

I quickly re-submitted a request to allow her exceptions to the command's movement control policies, citing the fresh specific statement of intent by the Commander of all U.S. Forces in Afghanistan. I was disheartened but not surprised to see NATO Training Mission - Afghanistan deny it outright. Sometimes three stars can trump four.

My quest for cultural attunement to become a more effective advisor led me to the game of Buzkashi and a book by G. Whitney Azoy called *Buzkashi – Game and Power in Afghanistan*.[14] Buzkashi is a national sport in Afghanistan that originated in the north. The game in its original form is played with a decapitated, de-hoofed goat carcass among any number of horse-mounted riders. The victor is the rider who can grab the goat and break away from the pack. The closest "game" in the U.S. to Buzkashi might be fumble-itis or "kill the guy with the football" where kids pick up the ball and run as fast as they can to get away from the other kids who are trying to tackle and strip the ball away so that they can grab it themselves and break away from the pack.

Buzkashi is a metaphor of Afghan politics and the struggle for power and control. The warlords or khans, would host the game, inviting rival khans to partake in the showcase of their marvelous stallions. While the rules are simple, applying the rules to the facts is always subject to interpretation. The game generates fast-paced excitement and plenty of disputes. The disputes generate as much, if not more, excitement than the game. Sometimes, disputes arise about the planning of the game, the second order game as described by Azoy. Sometimes it was about scoring: Was the horseman free and clear or was the pack gaining on him? This was the third-order game — the game of dispute resolution which brings prestige to the peacemaker or a slide into chaos and disgrace to the sponsor. Mr. Azoy's book made a number of invaluable observations of Afghan culture, verified by personal experience.

---

14 Azoy, G. Whitney, Buzkashi - Game and Power in Afghanistan. (Second Ed.) 2003 Waveland Press, Inc. The book is now available in a Third Edition.

An Afghan's greatest resource is individual reputation. Therefore, saving face is an important consideration when dealing with them. While helpful to find ways to allow saving face, it should not be an absolute maxim in all circumstances. Allowing an Afghan to save face must not be done in a way that shows weakness. While kindness will not always be mistaken for weakness, the gesture must be understood by the Afghan to be given from a position of strength and based on genuine friendship, or understandable business reasons. Genuine friendship is not likely to be achieved in the short tour of a Western advisor and it is always difficult to gauge what the Afghan understands to be sound business judgment. Therefore, strength tempered by restraint should be the basis of dealings with the Afghan.

Things are seldom what they seem in Afghanistan. The influential person in a position of power may, in fact, operate as a front for some more powerful and utterly silent man or network. Any given leader, from the president to minister to general, may not have the authority vested in the position that would be typical in the West. Many men perceived by the Westerner to be powerful, derive their power not from the institution, but from a khan or alliance of khans. Likewise, men of lower position in the eyes of the Westerner may wear a cloak of authority derived from a Khan, one that is clearly seen by the Afghans while invisible to the Westerner. I have seen junior ranking officers strike fear in the hearts of colonels and generals.

An Afghan's reputation is measured by success and spoils to be shared with his followers. This, of course, sheds light on the rampant corruption that occurs at all levels of the government and military, a "cultural framework" that undermines our mission in Afghanistan. This point is critical to understanding why our simplistic approach of throwing money at a problem will not succeed.

Individual Afghans struggle for control and seek to keep it for as long as they can hang on with no intent or planning for orderly succession. This undermines institutional development, career development and leadership development. A Western frame of reference for corporate and government institutions, features orderly, logical succession and continuity. It is a frame of reference ill-suited to understanding how Afghans do business. On a broad scale, one with gravitas cannot transfer it to another; either you have a name or not. The Western concept of delegated authority, successive authority and acting for the boss is alien for Afghans to understand, execute or follow.

Afghans are situational and agile, always hedging their bets and shifting alliances quickly. In conflict and victory, Afghans hedge their bets, anticipating that rivals could eventually become allies, and that allies may morph into rivals. A shift in political alignment leads followers to oppose friends, clients, enterprises, and policies of the predecessor.

These traits can have huge implications for the plight of U.S. - Afghan relations at every level. At the individual level, it has manifested tragically when trusted Afghan partners turned their weapons on their Western advisors and fellow fighters, incidents known as "Green on Blue" (Afghan Green on NATO Blue). This was a problem during my tour that made national headlines shortly after I left when an Afghan National Army Air Force Colonel killed nine U.S. Air Force personnel at a morning advisory meeting that took place at the Afghan Air Force base located at Kabul International Airport. At the national level, the scale of calamity could become disastrous. Appearances of friendship are indispensable to the Afghans, who seldom show enmity in the open and expertly hide their true alliances and motivations. Most Western advisors seemed to work with great dedication and trust, being mostly oblivious (culturally ignorant) to the inherent danger from close proximity to treacherous and possibly murderously psychotic Afghan leaders.

As in any culture, actions speak louder than words. When it comes to words, the Afghans make you work for every word of every sentence of every agreement. The Afghans embrace ambiguity and avoid specificity. Again, Dari, the northern Afghan language of universities, professionals and poets, is by Western standards an ambiguous language. The gravitation towards ambiguity and passive voice works against the Western desire for concise, precise agreements, regulations and procedures. Adjudication of seemingly simple concepts becomes complex.

In the game of Buzkashi, for example, with the simple goal of grabbing the carcass and then breaking free of the pack, the Toi must make a judgment call when declaring the horseman to be free of the others and thus the victor. Ambiguity also sets the stage for constant resetting of the clock, and robust arguments and re-negotiation of understandings and positions. Even when an Afghan leader makes a decision that seems to resolve an issue in dispute, another decision-maker may revise it in a subsequent step to demonstrate his control. Progress in Afghanistan that is measured in terms of agreements, written laws, regulations and promises, is the smallest measure of progress known to Western man.

Unbridled, chaotic, uninhibited, and at times uncontrolled competition lurks below the apparently cooperative surface. Dispute can become sport or much worse. Control over the dispute can become a goal because resolving a dispute between others can lend a patriarchal prestige to the reconciler – he has demonstrated control over chaos. Reconciliation after conflict is common. If the peacemaker is someone other than the organizer (of a Buzkashi match or other event), the peacemaker gains stature to the detriment of the organizer. This metaphor speaks directly to the Afghan insurgency and Pakistan's determination that reconciliation with the Taliban not occur without Pakistani control of the process.

For me, reading Azoy's book was akin to putting on prescription glasses for the first time to see the world in focus, especially the world where the easy is hard and the hard is easy. Now I understood a land where rivalries were so fierce that they moved the khans to bring vicious warfare to their land that included wanton decapitations, vulgar mastectomies for sport and cannibalism by trickery. Some Afghan Generals had relayed pre-Taliban stories from the 1990s of bands of warriors making "dancers" by decapitating rival tribe members as they stood helpless and flailing as the blood shot from their necks and others cutting off the breasts of women as they screamed in horror. Tajik Stew involves a tale of captured tribesmen being fed a stew of their fallen comrades, the identity of which was not revealed until dessert.

This is a land where under coalition leadership, tremendous resources flow from intended recipients into dark patronage networks; including some with business relationships with the very enemies to whom we lose sons, daughters, fathers and mothers. Where literally an Army of coalition colonels and generals work with the Afghan leaders for agreements and policies which are signed after a year-long negotiation, but never implemented because other Afghan leaders silently conclude such agreements and policies not to be in somebody's best interests.

One such document was known as "5001," the Manual of Organization and Functions. 5001 is the foundational regulatory scheme that establishes the structure and position responsibilities for command and control of the Afghan Army and Air Force. During my tour, the entire NATO Training Mission - Afghanistan Army Development team worked to rewrite 5001. The original 5001 had been developed during the command of U.S. Army Lieutenant General Formica. The Minister of Defense signed the document just before the end of General Formica's tour, and then put the document in his desk drawer and directed his subordinates to ignore it. It was apparently signed only to allow the American general to save face and show progress. At the end of my tour, the same Minister signed a new 5001 — just as the General Officers for Army Development were due to rotate. Was this progress or just another game of Buzkashi?

U.S. Air Force Colonel Greg Kleponis of Marple-Newtown, Pennsylvania in a Buzkashi Match

CHAPTER 10:
A MAN NEEDS A BIRD.

"Then some soldiers asked him, 'And what should we do?' He replied, 'Don't extort money and don't accuse people falsely — be content with your pay.'"

Luke 3:14

Corruption is widespread in Afghanistan, the topic of many studies, articles and high level missions by U.S. Leaders. It was given special attention by General Petraeus, who appointed Brigadier General H.R. McMaster to lead up a task force that would study and take action against corruption. H.R. McMaster is well known in military academic circles for his book, *Dereliction of Duty: Lyndon Johnson, Robert McNamara, The Joint Chiefs of Staff, and the Lies that Led to Vietnam.* The book stresses the importance of "speaking truth to power," words he used several times in conversation. H.R. McMaster was an enthusiastic leader without pretensions. The first time visiting his team at ISAF, I arrived early at their cramped cubicle filled basement space. His executive officer directed me to sit at a vacant cubicle while we talked and waited for H.R. When H.R. arrived, I realized the cubicle was his. He insisted that I sit tight. Unlike most Army generals in Kabul, there was no oversized, mahogany filled office for him. H.R. was a key member of General Petraeus' team that developed the Army's current counter-insurgency doctrine ("COIN"), which played a key role in the Iraq surge of 2007 and is being attempted in the current surge in Afghanistan.

The focus of counter-insurgency operations is the legitimacy of the host nation (Afghan) government.[15] One of the indicators of legitimacy is "a culturally acceptable level of corruption."[16] The first question a Western mind will ask is what level of corruption is acceptable? The better question to ask is: What do Afghans consider corruption?

Here is the best Afghan notion of corruption I came across during my tour: corruption is not sharing what you earn, beg, borrow or steal with your family, tribe and protector.

By that definition, the sky would seem to be the limit for corruption, making the Afghan government fully legitimate. However, by the same definition, for most of the Afghan population in and out of Kabul, the Afghan government is not sharing the largess lavished upon them by the American taxpayers, which of course would mean the government is illegitimate in the context of our counter-insurgency doctrine.

After taking command of ISAF, General Petraeus, looking for the "big idea" on corruption, stated that the best approach might be that of Secretary State Hillary Clinton: the U.S. will not tackle corruption everywhere, only where it impacts the Coalition's mission. Where might that line be? The reality is that corruption impacted and continues to impact all aspects of the Afghan government, and the Ministry of Defense was no exception. Corruption impacts recruiting, security, base and combat operations, land acquisition, promotions, contracting to feed, clothe, and

---

15 Army Field Manual 3-24, ¶1-113.

16 *Ibid*, ¶1-116.

equip soldiers, paying soldiers, transporting soldiers and even soldier medical care.

In the simplest terms, corruption undermined good order and discipline, essential to an effective army, which is essential to our counterinsurgency and exit strategy.

How do the Afghans, especially at the ministerial level, pull off rampant corruption while interfacing daily with ambassadors, generals and colonels? They know us better than we know them, especially the Afghans who fled to the U.S. when times were tough. Eventually, they returned to Afghanistan for "reconstruction" in much the same spirit of those who went to the U.S. southern states after our Civil War, toting bags made from old carpet to find their fortunes.

There's also the substitute teacher problem. The Afghans know that Coalition people, from generals to clerks in the State Department, are short-termers. The Afghans are in for the long haul – or at least until there are no more Western visitors bearing gifts.

It quickly became apparent that the Afghans were masters of white noise — sound that is so persistent, the mind blocks it out. The Afghans incessantly told stories of other Afghans' corruption. This was not a new phenomenon to the American Army. General Eisenhower spoke of it in 1942 when he was commanding Allied Forces in Algiers, which was a hot bed of corruption. "I sensed every individual was suspicious of everyone else - every man was sure all others were crooks and liars," Eisenhower said.[17] The Afghans knew that stories of corruption pushed a hot button with the Coalition, especially the new officers. With turnover of Coalition positions at least once a year for most, and six months for others, there were always plenty of new Coalition officers to taunt and to pit against rivals and friends. Sometimes it seemed like a sport — a Buzkashi. To many Coalition officers, the Afghan reports of corruption became a joke, not to be taken seriously. They became white noise.

---

17 (Eisenhower: A Soldier's Life, Carlo D'Este p 364.)

Another drag on the Coalition's ability to curb corruption was what might be likened to Stockholm Syndrome. Stockholm Syndrome occurs when hostages bond with their captors, feeling gratitude and even loyalty or affection towards them. In the advisory context, the advisor knows corruption abounds, but the specific Afghan to whom the advisor is assigned is not corrupt because the advisor has gotten to know him well.

As a professional investigator of embezzlement schemes in civilian life, I have been vaccinated to a large degree from this syndrome, having learned that the "con" in con-man stands for the "confidence" he instills in his victims, not "convict" as some might think. Conmen succeed because they become well known to their victims, gaining their trust. Many of my fellow advisors, mostly intelligence officers and Special Forces, were likewise resistant to the syndrome. Unfortunately, there were many colonels and generals whose narrow experience in life made them susceptible. Indeed, they are in good company. It is believed that Ulysses S. Grant, one of America's greatest generals, whose presidential administration was rife with scandal, was ill-prepared by his American Army experience for dealing with vultures. He was accustomed to being surrounded by men of virtue whose word he could take at face value. But when dealing with scoundrels, Grant was made to look a fool. In Afghanistan, it often seemed like we sent Boy Scouts to give resources and advice to the Sopranos.

In early 2010, the Coalition announced its intention to expel the Taliban from Kandahar in a massive operation to be called Hamkari. Kandahar was the birthplace of the Taliban and home of Mullah Omar, a.k.a. the one-eyed mullah who embraced Osama Bin Laden and his terrorist training camps. The Afghan National Army was to fight "shoulder-to-shoulder" or "shona ba shona" with U.S., British, Canadian and Australian forces, thus putting an Afghan face on the operation and demonstrating progress in the development of Afghan Security forces.

However, this initiative faced a critical challenge: the Afghan National Army suffered from exceedingly high AWOL rates in the south where the fighting was most fierce and would intensify. While seeking a solution to the problem, one AWOL soldier stood out like a sore thumb. A Staff Judge Advocate, the chief legal officer responsible for the administration of justice and discipline at one of the key Afghan Corps ("General X"), was AWOL and had been so since his appointment in November 2009.

When I asked about General X, Afghan legal officers in Kabul informed me that he was illiterate and had been removed from a garrison command because of gross inattention to duties, corruption and incompetence. Because of his ties to powerful people, the Afghan leadership gave him high rank and position in the Army, placing him in the Staff Judge Advocate position where they felt he could do the least amount of harm. These Afghan Legal officers referred to General X as a wealthy and powerful man, as well as smuggler and pseudo-godfather who showered locals with Sport Utility Vehicles and other lavish gifts in the manner of Pablo Escobar.

When I expressed disbelief, the Afghans made a comment I would hear many times: "Now you see the problems we have in Afghanistan."

There was a bright side to General X's absence from duty. At least he was not meddling in legal affairs for which he was unqualified. Instead, the Afghans lamented, he was busy tending to his lucrative business as a contracted security provider to the Coalition.

Trying to report General X to the Coalition chain of command resulted in a response typical for allegations of corruption and misdeeds: there needs to be proof to present to the Afghan leadership. Your job is not to fight corruption or collect information but to build ministries. "Stay in your lane. Be correctors, not collectors," I was told.

But the rule of law was my team's "lane" and our Afghans were the ones with the mission to enforce the rule of law against corruption within the Ministry of Defense. So, we decided to use General X as our test in empowering the rule of law within the Ministry of Defense.

We set out to find out more about the AWOL Staff Judge Advocate. Were the stories about him true? Was he really absent, drawing pay, and hopelessly unqualified and illiterate? Was he the benefactor of patronage, and if so, who was his true patron given the Afghans' mastery of hiding alliances and grievances? If we could answer these questions with evidence, then maybe we could bring some Coalition pressure on the Afghan leadership, perhaps making an example that could become the starting point for the rule of law to take hold within the Afghan Army.

General X's corps commander confirmed to our team what we had heard from a local Coalition advisor, General X had been AWOL for seven months since his appointment. We also learned he had been drawing pay. The corps commander repeated what had been said earlier: General X was too busy with his contracting business providing security to the Coalition. When asked why he tolerated this, the commander arched his eyebrows and said, "What can I do? He has friends." He pointed to Karzai's picture.

Like all the Afghan commanders I met, he repeated the same passionate anti-corruption creed. Corruption in the government was clearly worse than five years ago. The government does not have the support of the people because the government does not place competent people in positions that serve the people. This may be strengthening the Taliban. The local prosecutor in Kandahar City is incompetent, does not move cases and causes the people to turn to the Taliban for justice. Corruption was a serious problem and had to be dealt with at levels higher than him so the fix would work its way down.

The commander expressed frustration with Coalition leadership for ignoring corruption within the Afghan National Army and the Afghan Government. He seemed like a forthright man. But alas, this was Afghanistan.

Interestingly, there were also numerous accusations of corruption against the same corps commander who had complained to me about the corrosive effects of corruption. Like every other Afghan general I met, the claims included tales of money and gifts flowing to him. More white noise? The Afghan legal generals insisted the accusations against General X were correct. Why then, had they not pushed for his removal? The law on the books gave the Chief of GS Legal the authority to remove officers in legal positions. I raised the issue day after day through many cups of tea and bowls of nuts and raisins and a carton of second hand smoke. After several meetings, one of the generals snapped at me for pushing him so hard to take action against General X. "Why should I do anything when the Coalition does nothing to stop corruption?," he complained.

The response I gave was the Coalition stock answer for a "corrector": The Coalition can't fix this problem; it requires an Afghan solution. You need to do the right thing. The tirade that followed at once surprised and impressed me:

"I am tired of hearing mentors tell us about Afghan solutions! If you want to see what Afghan solutions look like, look at this country in 2001! All of the destruction and endless fighting, that is what Afghan solutions bring! You are here because we need your help. But you bring large amounts of money to this country that is not used to having money. You let people steal this money, accumulate power. You do nothing to stop it. We can't help it, we will steal until you stop us. You feed this problem and you must help to stop it. The Army before the Taliban used to have discipline. Even though it was poorer, with less material and buildings, morale was good. Commanders used to live with their soldiers and those that broke the law were punished. Now, commanders make money. They do not live with their soldiers. They build large houses for themselves and the soldiers and Afghan people see this. Commanders cannot be punished because they are protected by their party or powerful men. You must be part of the solution!"

Initially defensive, I realized "you" was not me. It was a reference to the Coalition and the U.S. in particular. I assured the general of my commitment to help him and Afghan National Army GS Legal implement the rule of law. I explained how I put myself in danger to do so, how my daughter cried learning that her father was going to a place where anyone could be shot or blown up by a suicide bomber. In turn, Afghanistan needed men willing to put not only their life but also their jobs at stake. My promise was to push Coalition leadership to empower the rule of law, but that Afghan National Army Legal needed to get in front and lead, bringing the issue to the feet of powerful men and giving the Coalition the opportunity to confront and correct them through the rule of law.

The exchange caused me to reflect on my first day of being introduced to the Afghan leadership. A colleague had asked General Nooristani whether corruption in Afghanistan was worse under the Soviets or the Coalition. His response took all of us by surprise: Under the coalition, of course. Having heard so much about the Afghan's hatred for the Russians and our own Cold War frame of reference to the "Evil Empire," we all tilted our heads like Golden Retrievers wondering what happened to the ball we thought was coming our way. The general explained that the Communists did not bring money to Afghanistan, so the opportunities for corruption were far fewer.

Things started to make more sense.

General Petraeus has said more than once that in a counterinsurgency, money is ammunition. Like a World War I artillery barrage that laid so many shells into the European countryside that unexploded munitions still surface every spring to this day, the U.S. has bombarded Afghanistan with the ammunition of money. And just as with traditional ammunition, there is collateral damage.

In Afghanistan, a population not used to wealth and currency and with no vision beyond this week, using resources on anyone other than one's immediate family, tribe and protector was unthinkable, no matter how much the West talked about building a better Afghanistan. I thought back to the stories of soldiers who came upon the starving masses at Nazi concentration camps. Their natural inclination was to feed these victims of inhumanity. But physicians had to stop them, lest they kill the freed prisoners by shocking their systems with too much food too fast. The Coalition had been doing the same thing from the earliest days of the conflict.

I thought of a story I heard Johnny Carson tell, which seemed to fit the lessons being learned, which coincidentally involved a dog. It was my turn to tell a story to an Afghan general:

> This man had a dog trained to fetch him vodka from the kitchen. Even more impressive was that, when the vodka was gone, this man could put five dollars under the dog's collar and direct him to the liquor store. The dog would faithfully go to the store and come back with a new bottle of vodka. One day, the man only had a 20 dollar bill, so he put it under the dog's collar with a note to the clerk instructing him to put the change under the dog's collar. Hours went by and the dog failed to return home with the vodka. The man went to the store, asking for his dog. The clerk replied that the dog had been there hours ago to buy vodka and cigarettes. Cigarettes?! The man continued his search and finally came across his dog in a field, lying with a bitch, both smoking cigarettes next to an empty bottle of vodka. The man shouted to his dog, "What are you doing? Where is my change!" The dog responded that there was no change. The vodka was five dollars; the cigarettes were five dollars; and, he had to give the rest of the money to the bitch. "I don't understand this," the dog's owner said. "You were always so loyal, never corrupt!" The dog replied, "You never gave me 20 dollars before."

The general smiled as he put out his cigarette. "Now you understand the problems we have in Afghanistan," he said.

The Chief of GS Legal issued a memo to the Afghan National Army G1 (personnel) that detailed the AWOL Staff Judge Advocate's absence from duty and his lack of qualifications for the position, requesting his removal. The G1 responded, that despite the law, he would take no action, the Minister of Defense must do so. The newly appointed Deputy Minister of Defense, himself a lawyer, former chief prosecutor, and the first true civilian to occupy a high level position in the Ministry of Defense, readily agreed to take up the cause. He promised with a smile to have General X removed immediately. From his perspective, the law was clear and he would see to it.

Days later, the Deputy was visibly chagrined. General X could not be removed. Although the Deputy Minister did not explain why, his boss' Coalition advisors provided partial explanation: The Minister of Defense insisted that GS Legal had its facts all wrong about the AWOL Staff Judge Advocate. The Minister did not like lawyers because U.S. lawyers recently blocked U.S. reimbursement of his expenses from a recent trip to Malaysia.

We would have only one more opportunity to make General X an example.

Twice a month, the Army advisors met at the Ministry of Defense with our Afghan counterparts to brief key issues of the day. Armed with a little knowledge about the Afghan's love of stories and pictures, an observer of these PowerPoint-centric meetings would conclude they were held more to appease the Coalition than to make an impact on the Afghan National Army.

At one such meeting, my interpreters did not have the time to finish translating my PowerPoint slides into Dari, so I used some photographs of young legal recruits in training as a way to discuss the Afghan National Army Legal's recruiting and training efforts. Not surprisingly, the Afghans actually paid attention and looked at the slides while I briefed, instead of the more common 100-inch-stare into the table that crosses cultural boundaries when it comes to the overuse of PowerPoint.

One of these meetings presented an opportunity to pursue an Afghan solution to the AWOL Staff Judge Advocate problem and to portray how General X represented what was wrong with Afghanistan. It came my turn to brief and I asked all of the generals in the room to make this their issue for their army, for their soldiers, for their country:

> This man represents all that is wrong with Afghanistan. He is
> in a professional position, but he is not an educated man. He
> is in a law enforcement position, but he is a criminal who takes
> pay without serving. He calls himself a soldier, but he does
> not even show for duty. He wants to wear the same uniform
> that brave young Afghans have worn fighting and dying for
> Afghanistan, but he does not deserve to wear the uniform of
> heroes. Each of you are leaders of this Army and you need to
> push yourselves and your leaders to stop this. Start with this
> man and remove him.

The words rolled off my tongue. I almost felt my body swaying as I seemed to rise above it, looking down at myself and others in the room. I could see the Afghan generals stare ahead or down, showing no signs of confusion or understanding. A U.S. Air Force Colonel logistics advisor pumped his arm in the air and another moved his eyes from side to side seeming to wonder if he should be chambering a round into his weapon. When I finished, an Afghan National Army sergeant major leaped from his chair and ran out of the room. Later, I learned that he ran to call his U.S. advisor, to tell him of this great speech he just heard and how shamefully silent the Afghan generals were in response.

Shortly thereafter, the new Chief of Staff of the Afghan Army asked me what three things he could do to help strengthen the law within the Army. One of the things I asked him to do was to insist that the Army follow the existing law that empowers the Chief of GS Legal to both assign and remove officers in legal positions. The Chief smiled and said in near-perfect English, "I know you are speaking of General X. I know he is not an educated man, but you must understand that this is political. He came to my office yesterday to discuss this situation. He said he does not even want the position of Staff Judge Advocate; he wants to be a commander. But he is a friend of President Karzai; he fought with him against the Russians. He cannot be removed. The good news, however, is that he is very rich. He even spends his money on his unit. So, we do not have to worry about corruption with him."

In the U.S. Army, it would seem insane to even contemplate the possibility that an illiterate wealthy man in one of the poorest, largest drug trafficking countries in the world is not corrupt because he spreads his wealth among his unit members. But we had stepped through the looking glass and into Wonderland. This was Afghanistan, the land in between. Three months later, "good news" came: General X had been promoted to commander of a garrison, clearing the way for a real lawyer to be assigned as Staff Judge Advocate.

Through yet another thick cloud of cigarette smoke, an Afghan general told a story of a man that needed a bird.

This man went to a bazaar where he found Karzai, a Pashtun of the Popalzai clan. Karzai stood there in his royal green jacket with a bird perched on each shoulder and one on the ridge of his wool Karzai hat. "Those are beautiful birds" said the man. "How much for this bird on your left shoulder?"

Karzai replied: "Ten Thousand Afghani."

"That is a lot of money for a bird," the man responded. "Why so much?"

Karzai answered: "This bird can speak Dari and Pashto."

So, the man asked: "How much for the bird on your right shoulder?"

Karzai said: "He costs 20,000 Afghani. He speaks Dari, Pashto and English."

"I am afraid to ask how much the bird on your head costs" uttered the man.

Karzai said firmly "He is 50,000 Afghani."

"For that price, surely he must write and read all three languages," replied the man.

Karzai retorted: "No, this bird cannot read, write or speak any language. But he is Popalzai and he is the boss of the other two birds!"

Except for the few times that the Afghan legal officers would mention General X as a supreme example of the futility of applying the rule of law within the Ministry of Defense and the Afghan National Army, General X became an issue of the past, a bridge too far to cross.

After I left Afghanistan, while waiting at Fort Benning to be cleared for my final trek home, an Afghan on his way to Kandahar as a contract interpreter asked me of my impressions of the situation in his homeland. When I told him of the problems with fake doctors, fake lawyers and fake generals, he became animated: "Like that IDIOT General X from Kandahar!" "You know General X?," I asked. "Of course," the interpreter replied. "He is an idiot. He cannot even read, but he puts on his uniform and says I am a general!"

Sadly, General X was not an exception. An uneducated Afghan corps commander was promoted despite evidence that he had beaten and jailed a subordinate to the point of internal bleeding. He was being considered for an even bigger position in the Afghan Army. The day before being recalled to the states by President Obama because of the infamous Rolling Stone article, General McCrystal met with President Karzai, armed with my team's report. He helped persuade President Karzai to promote the thug to a lower position. That the investigation took place at all was "measured progress" and a testament to the combined courage of a young Afghan lawyer, a Coalition legal advisor and the Chief of GS Legal who had pushed the matter.

Playing a role in blocking this general from the bigger promotion was a mini cause célèbre. But even that small celebration was cut short when the Afghan lawyers reviewed evidence that the general stole $8,000 from his corps, possibly to pay what one Afghan officer described as the customary bribe for processing promotion paperwork. Despite documentary evidence and the word of the Corps Deputy Commander, Finance Officer and Deputy Staff Judge Advocate, the Ministry of Defense and Afghan National Army leadership either would not or could not do anything about this general's misconduct. Likewise, the Coalition leadership did nothing to correct the situation. What could they do? This is Afghanistan. The corps commander got another star.

Even fuel fueled corruption. Afghan bases were filled with wrecked vehicles, purchased by U.S. taxpayers. These wrecks remained active on the units' books so commanders could continue drawing fuel and selling it on the black market. One weak attempt to combat the pilfering of fuel was to dye it blue and let Afghans know that they should not possess, purchase or sell blue fuel. I accept that somewhere in Afghanistan, there is probably a person who would be deterred from possessing, purchasing, or selling blue fuel, but that person remains known only to God. Many generators lie idle for hours — not because of a lack of fuel, but a lack of discipline that allows commanders to divert and sell the fuel intended to take care of their troops.

The same happens with food, weapons, and even medicine.

Soldiers trying to get home for the holidays have been stranded as victims of "hot ticketing." Hot ticketing occurs when pilots of Afghan military aircraft sell their passenger and cargo space to the highest bidder, often not the dirt-poor junior soldiers of the Afghan National Army and their families. One such incident was captured on a surveillance video and showed young family members entitled to transport being harshly pulled out of their seats and shoved off the aircraft. This video led to the court-martial of a pilot who was connected to one of the dark networks within the Ministry of Defense. Credible death threats against the key witness almost stopped the trial from moving forward. The senior prosecutors refused to take the case, which was dumped on the most junior lieutenant recently out of school. In his closing argument, in complete violation of Afghan prosecutorial procedure, he strenuously argued for leniency for the Afghan Air Force colonel because he was a good man that should not be defined by one bad incident. The pilot was given a sentence of six-month's probation with his unit.

Even murder has been excused by the Afghan leadership. In one region of Afghanistan, an Afghan National Army soldier shot a twelve-year-old girl in the head, killing her instantly. The corps commander refused to initiate an investigation. The Brigade Commander of the shooter and his G1 (personnel officer) appeared to have paved the way for the soldier from their tribe to flee the area before an investigation might take place. The first story fed up the chain of command was that the girl was caught in the cross-fire between Afghan National Army and Taliban. The Chief of General Staff focused on that story and did not react with indignation at the corps commander's inexcusable decision not to have an investigation.

When it quickly came to light that there were no reports of fighting in the area, the story changed. The girl popped up from behind a bush and startled the soldier, who fired his weapon, killing her. While that story was being told to authorities, a young Afghan lieutenant blurted out that he could not take this any longer and said that the soldier and two others were trying to rape the girl. She resisted, so one of the soldiers placed a gun to her head and it "went off." The field grade officer present started yelling at the young lieutenant, warning that he was going to get them all in trouble. Although Coalition legal advisors were able to force an investigation of the incident, the Afghan National Army delayed, slow-rolled, and avoided investigating the cover-ups in the chain of command. In a responsible, disciplined military, the Corps and Brigade Commanders would have been relieved of command.

Corruption did not limit its reach to the Ministry of Defense. It polluted the Afghan National Police (ANP) to the point that they are viewed as predatory thugs by the Afghan people. One advisor to a senior Afghan leader in the Ministry of Interior, which is the "civilian" ministry overseeing the paramilitary Afghan National Police, spent much time on the road inspecting Afghan National Police posts. At one post, the policemen complained that they only had electricity and hot water one hour per day. The generator operator explained that he was only given enough fuel to operate it one hour per day. The U.S. taxpayers provided more than enough fuel to run the generator all day. What happened to the rest of the fuel? The commander also collected the policemen's daily food stipends, compelling them to eat in the unit "dining facility," which consisted of a dirty pot with swill that was barely edible.

But the most despicable effects of corruption that came to light during my tour fell upon the wounded, young Afghan soldiers and their families.

CHAPTER 11:
PHYSICIAN, HEAL THYSELF

"You who choose to lead must follow."

Robert Hunter

A senior U.S. officer privately observed:

"I'm routinely amazed at how obnoxiously assertive officers can be with their subordinates and peers and then turn into complete invertebrates (i.e., no backbone) when they address their superiors."[18]

Many who have observed Afghan officers would agree with the comment. However, the quote describes not Afghans, but U.S. Army officers and can be found in a U.S. Army War College Publication. The U.S. Army has become concerned about the prevalence and effects of "toxic"

---

18 Stephen J. Gerras, Leonard Wong, Charles D. Allen, Organizational Culture: Applying A Hybrid Model to the U.S. Army, U.S. Army War College November 2008

leadership.[19] Toxic leadership was alive and not well at NATO Training Mission – Afghanistan. It explains how the military reports progress in Afghanistan while those close to the ground see dismal conditions everywhere they look.

The Army defines toxic leaders as commanders who put their own needs first, micro-manage subordinates, behave in a mean-spirited manner or display poor decision making.[20] In a recent survey discussed in the *Washington Post*, more than 80% of Army officers and sergeants had directly observed a "toxic" leader in the last year. About 20% of the respondents said that they had worked directly for one. The survey also found that 97% of officers and sergeants had observed an "exceptional leader" within the Army in the past year.[21] While there was exceptional leadership at NATO Training Mission - Afghanistan, it was sparse among U.S. Army general officers.

Toxic leadership can impact the mission in many ways. In addition to degrading morale, it creates an environment where subordinates are reluctant to report information that runs contrary to what leadership wants to hear. This, in turn, undermines the accurate assessment and critical thinking needed to make good decisions that foster mission accomplishment. Where the mission is to train and advise another nation's military in the ways of the profession of arms, it can undermine the moral standing of the trainers who are trying to instill professionalism and create an atmosphere conducive to selfless service subordinate to the rule of law, the glue of a stable society. Most importantly, it can lead to an erosion of trust between the people and their military.

A can-do attitude is the cornerstone of success in military or business endeavors. Where weaker men might fail, the Army produces leaders and followers that possess the personal and moral courage that keep it

---

19 Army worries about 'toxic leaders' in ranks By Greg Jaffe, Published: June 25, 2011

20 Ibid.

21 Ibid.

rolling along. Commitment to success includes a covenant that, if necessary, you will give your life or ability to see, walk, sleep or love, in exchange
for victory. That someone is willing to put so much on the line for success
is a measure of how strong the desire for success burns inside.

One sacrifice that many officers seem unwilling to make is their
career. This is not unique to the military by any means. People who have
worked in corporate America know the phenomena too well. However,
it is hard to imagine any of the corporate ladder climbers with flexible
ethics willing to sacrifice anything near what the soldier puts on the line.
In that regard, the military officer stands head and shoulders above the
businessman. However, the consequences of an officer unwilling to tolerate challenges or being reluctant to speak up are more profound. For
a businessman, displaying an agreeable can-do attitude without question
can mean continued membership in the inner circle and collection of rich
rewards while the company drifts towards financial ruin. For an officer, it
can mean good ratings by the boss, but also unnecessary loss of life, mission failure, loss of national prestige or the breakdown of trust between
the military and its people. Trust, when broken, as it was after the Vietnam
conflict, can take decades to restore. Trust is the bedrock of the all-volunteer Army and its sacred bond with our Nation.

It is incumbent on leaders at every level to go beyond lip service
and take affirmative action to encourage dissent and spirited debate where
time and place allows. In a speech to West Point Cadets in April 2008, U.S.
Secretary of Defense Robert Gates said:

I encourage you to take on the mantle of fearless, thoughtful, but
loyal dissent when the situation calls for it. And agree with the articles or
not, senior officers should embrace such dissent as healthy dialogue and
protect and advance those considerably more junior who are taking on
that mantle.[22]

---

22 Robert M. Gates, "Evening Lecture at the U.S. Military Academy," lecture, United
States Military Academy at West Point, 21 April, 2008.

On the traditional battlefield, tactical decisions don't allow it. But in today's complex environments like Afghanistan, where "money is ammunition" and host nation officials can be deceitful, self-interested and defiant, critical thinking and candid reporting of capabilities and limitations are essential.

One example of how toxic leadership impacted the mission is the state of the Afghan National Army's healthcare system. The United States has poured hundreds of millions of dollars into the system with little benefit to the Afghan soldier or the Coalition mission of enhancing the Afghan government's legitimacy.

NATO Training Mission - Afghanistan developed a rating system to measure the status and progress of the Afghan National Army and its subsystems. In early 2010, NATO Training Mission - Afghanistan upgraded the rating of the Afghan National Army medical system from CM4 (Coalition does it for them, complete support) to CM3 (Coalition does it with them but mentoring/advisory input required). As late as February 2010, NATO Training Mission - Afghanistan reported on its website (www. NTM-A.com) a number of stories touting the successful development of "enduring medical systems in the Afghan National Army." One article spoke of the successful medical logisticians course for the Afghan National Army. The ceremony was presided over by the Afghan National Army Surgeon General Yaftali, who "noted that this course represents a new phase in Afghan National Army training, the first time that the Afghan National Army will have officers specifically trained in [medical logistics], allowing doctors to dedicate their time to taking care of patients." The article continued: "The NATO Training Mission and Combined Security Transition Command – Afghanistan Medical Training Advisory Group is proud to support the Afghan National Security Forces in developing enduring medical training capacity for the people of Afghanistan."

You can find many articles about the great successes of NATO Training Mission - Afghanistan's efforts with regard to all aspects of the building of Afghanistan's security forces.

But the view on the ground seemed much different from the rosy pictures portrayed by the officers eager to blog the good news sought by the command.

Many millions were spent on the ANA's medical system. The official assessment reported to the National Command Authority and to Congress was that the system was able to function with advisors' assistance. However, the field would report that military doctors and nurses were not treating Afghan soldiers with medicine and were refusing to report for duty in the south where fighting was most intense and the need for health care providers was greatest. Ground-level reports included Afghans performing surgery on Afghan soldiers without morphine in a land that is the world's opium dealer. NATO commanders responsible for Afghan National Army units fighting in the field would complain about the lack of medicine and demand supplies. NATO Training Mission - Afghanistan continued to procure large quantities of medicine, but the complaints from the field continued.

At one point, Afghan National Army officials asked me to have NATO Training Mission - Afghanistan provide an official tally of how many pharmaceuticals we had supplied to the Afghan National Army. Initial numbers provided by the Medical Training Advisory Group (MTAG) were staggering. It appeared from the amount of medical support provided by the Coalition, almost all of it financed by the U.S. taxpayers, that there was a gross leak in the system. The MTAG also provided some historical information that, based on my experience investigating embezzlement and kickback schemes, raised flags about possible fraud waste and abuse on the side of the Coalition. There were also accusations of the same by some Afghan generals who were not suspected of being involved in the fraud. Finally, when three different arms of the Combined Security Transition Command - Afghanistan provided three different numbers regarding the amount of medical support provided by the U.S. to the Afghan National Army, it seemed appropriate that procurement practices be scrutinized.

The words of a Contract Attorney instructor at the U.S. Army JAG School echoed in my head through the decades: If you see evidence of fraud, waste and abuse, you call the fraud, waste and abuse hotline.

Working with the NATO Training Mission - Afghanistan Command Inspector General, I delivered a written summary of the problem and my concerns regarding fraud, waste and abuse. It is important to understand that the Afghans do not corner the market on fraud and corruption. Some Afghans and Americans were quick to dismiss concerns about Afghan corruption by pointing out that corruption exists everywhere, even in the U.S. But the difference between Afghanistan and the U.S. is that here there is a constant effort to contain, expose and punish corruption. Corruption is like a bathroom. If you don't persistently clean your bathroom, it gets disgusting. In Afghanistan, the Afghans make little effort to clean their bathrooms or their corruption.

There have been documented instances of fraud, waste and abuse by Americans in the U.S. war efforts in Iraq and Afghanistan. There has been a Special Inspector General for Afghan Reconstruction (SIGAR) to investigate such matters in Afghanistan and similar investigations for Iraq. One officer from my old Civil Affairs unit was convicted of taking kickbacks from a contractor in Iraq and was sentenced to 30 months in prison. If an Afghan made an accusation of corruption against Coalition personnel, I was not as quick to dismiss it as many others seemed to be. On one occasion where Afghan officials made a colorable accusation of corruption against a Coalition officer, I worked quietly with local U.S. Criminal Investigation Division (CID) officials to rule it out. With the new accusations by Afghans and red flags independent of the accusations, going to the Command Inspector General seemed compelling.

The NATO Training Mission - Afghanistan Command Inspector General had the traditional inspector general function of taking complaints and investigating them, which in itself was a full-time job. He was also responsible for advising both the Afghan National Army Inspector General and Afghan National Police Inspector General. His staff travelled to four locations each day to train the Afghan IGs. He stated he did not have the capacity or expertise to conduct an investigation of the medical situation, but agreed there was a need to do so.

Having received numerous complaints of corruption bleeding Coalition resources in many other Afghan departments, he thought it prudent to recommend that the command bring in a team from the Department of Defense Inspector General that specialized in medical logistics fraud waste and abuse to investigate. As fellow advisors, we thought it would be an excellent opportunity not only to have an investigation of our internal procurement and delivery practices, but also to demonstrate to the Afghans that we practice the transparency and accountability we had been preaching in our advisory roles. It also presented an opportunity to have the Department of Defense Inspector General partner with the Ministry of Defense Inspector General to investigate the problems with the ANA's medical logistics. The U.S. recently had started a program of having Department of Defense civilians deploy to Afghanistan to advise their civilian counterparts in the Ministry of Defense and this opportunity seemed to fit the bill in every respect.

It is important to understand the limits of U.S. law and jurisdiction or authority over the Afghans when it comes to money and materials we have donated to them. Once the delivery is made, the donation becomes property of the Afghan government. Any misuse or theft of such property by Afghans is not a violation of U.S. law and the Afghan perpetrators are not subject to U.S. investigatory powers. In setting up the new Afghan government, no treaty was entered into that would give the U.S. such authority.

This reality is what has made U.S. efforts to deal with Afghan corruption such a Catch-22. When the U.S. receives intelligence that Afghans are pilfering U.S. donations and undermining NATO counter-insurgency efforts to legitimize the Afghan government, that same government demands proof that is admissible in the Afghan legal system. Intelligence is not proof sufficient for that purpose.

The Afghan government will typically "conduct their investigation" and determine that U.S. allegations were wrong. When asked to see the details of an investigation or to assist with it, the Afghan government declares that such requests are insults to their sovereignty and they consider the matter closed. When pushed hard diplomatically, the head of the Afghan government, Karzai, throws tantrums. In early 2010, he declared that he might join the Taliban. In October 2011, he assured Pakistan that he would side with them against the U.S. should the U.S. attack Pakistan. This leaves the U.S. with one of two choices: make more donations or stop making donations.

To stop making donations to the Afghan government, whose tax collections total $1 billion dollars a year, would mean allowing the immediate collapse of the Afghan Security Forces, which are sustained by U.S. taxpayers at the rate of almost $1 billion a month. To date, when the Afghan government tells the U.S. Government "Shut up and give me more money," the U.S. has sheepishly responded, "OK, please don't let us fail in making you legitimate to your own people. Please do something about the pilfering."

Understanding the "rules of engagement" when using money as ammunition is also important. In general, there is an understanding that not all money spent in a hostile fire area will hit its target. While stewardship is encouraged, there is an understanding that in war zones, not all of the checks and balances present in a domestic environment can or should apply. The commander is given more latitude in spending that money. An analogy that some will argue with is Medicare. In the U.S., Medicare's purpose is to provide access to healthcare services and goods to the elderly. Because of the intended beneficiaries often require rapid attention, the government makes the system easy to use. This ease of use makes the system susceptible to bleeding by unscrupulous crooks. The more restrictions placed on Medicare to counter fraud, the less it will reach its intended audience. Therefore, some leakage is expected with Medicare.

The same is true with counter-insurgency funding. The question becomes, how much ammunition money should be hitting the target? If little to none is hitting the target, at what point does it exceed acceptable leakage, becoming waste or abuse instead?

The Command Inspector General decided to brief the NATO Training Mission - Afghanistan Command Group to alert them to the serious problem and of the need to bring the Department of Defense Inspector General medical logistics team to Kabul. The NATO Training Mission - Afghanistan Chief of Staff directed him to the civilian Deputy to the Commander for the briefing.

On October 27, 2010, the Inspector General presented his briefing in the presence of the Command Staff Judge Advocate, Chief Advisor for Counter Corruption, the Command Surgeon and Medical Advisor and myself. He opined that a Department of Defense Inspector General investigation into the irregularities of the procurement and delivery of medical supplies to the Afghan National Army was essential. Once the meds are transferred to Afghan ownership, U.S. law has no say over what should happen to them. The meds belong to the Afghan government and if an Afghan steals them, it is Afghan law that is broken. There is no American jurisdiction to investigate or prosecute

The Command IG argued that the Department of Defense IG should partner with the Afghans to determine what happened to the endless supplies once given to the Afghan National Army. The Deputy declared this to be a "no brainer" and directed the Command IG to make the request for the Department of Defense IG to send a team. The Command IG quickly made contact with Ambassador Kenneth P. Moorefield of the Department of Defense IG Special Plans and Operations division. He invited me to sit in on a video conference call the next day with folks in Washington to help them prepare for their trip to Kabul.

After the video conference call, Lieutenant General Caldwell returned to Camp Eggers and learned of the decision to bring in the Department of Defense Inspector General. I got word that he was livid with his Deputy and Inspector General. Caldwell was said to be concerned about the timing coming on the eve of the U.S. congressional elections. Later that Friday night, the Deputy Commander for Army Training and Development, then Brigadier General Gary Patton, convened a meeting to discuss the Department of Defense Inspector General's request. The Command Inspector General was not present. Patton informed the group that Lieutenant General Caldwell was upset about making the request so close to the election. He told us we were to consider postponing it until afterwards. There was much discussion about the substance of the prob-lem; how to present the facts of the Department of Defense Inspector General visit to the Afghans; whether to disclose the problems with the Afghan National Army medical system to allies contemplating donations; and, whether the request for an investigation should be changed to an assistance visit.

Again, General Patton mentioned the elections. I felt compelled to voice concern about the inappropriateness of allowing such considerations into the decision-making process. I made it clear that I was not at the meeting as a legal advisor to the Command Group and that my comments were not legal advice but simply words grounded in a tradition that mili-tary officers should neither make decisions based on politics nor allow an appearance of such. I urged General Patton to consider how he would answer questions posed by U.S. Senators regarding decisions made with political considerations. The discussion of the elections also made no sense because the request was staying within the Department of Defense and would sit dormant over the weekend. By the time it began internal staffing, the election would be over.

We concluded the meeting with guidance on how to present the issue to the Afghans and very clear instructions that if the effort moved forward, it will be a request for a Department of Defense Inspector General Assistance Visit, not an investigation. The next day, Saturday, the Command Inspector General was directed to pull back the request to Department of Defense Inspector General.

After the U.S. elections of November 2, 2010, a meeting was called in Caldwell's office. Although not invited to this meeting, its events were relayed to me by three officers who were there and all three descriptions were in sync. Caldwell screamed at these three officers, waving his finger at them for trying to bring in the Department of Defense Inspector General. "You are all O6s (the pay grade for Colonels and Naval Captains) and should know better. There is nothing wrong in this command that we can't fix ourselves," He said. To the great credit and moral courage of these officers, they stood their ground and insisted that bringing in the Department of Defense Inspector General was appropriate and necessary. As a result, Lieutenant General Caldwell directed that Assistant Commanding General for Army Development, then Brigadier General David Neasmith, examine the issue and make a recommendation to him on whether a request to the Department of Defense Inspector General should proceed.

A recently arrived colonel, who was not familiar with, and therefore not "tainted" by, the dynamics of the relationships between the Coalition and the Afghan advisees, was tasked to lead this phase. Several meetings took place, and at times debate was heated. During this process, the Command Inspector General received numerous complaints from members of the U.S. Medical Training Advisory Group (MTAG) of horrid conditions at the Afghan National Military Hospital in Kabul, the "crown jewel" of the Afghan National Army medical system. In his capacity as advisor to the Ministry of Defense Inspector General, he began a series of joint inspections of the National Military Hospital with the Afghan Inspector General.

What he saw was horrifying. Patients were lying in filth, in some cases starving and suffering from grotesque bed sores. One starving patient, who was on the brink of death, became known to the advisory team as "Patient Zero." Sadly, despite intense efforts led by the U.S. Medical Advisory Group to save him, Patient Zero died. It was the Ministry of Defense Inspector General who disclosed that Afghan doctors and nurses would not tend to a patient unless he came from their clan or they were able to pay gratuities for the care. Most of the doctors and nurses, all officers of the Afghan National Army, would only show up to work from 10 a.m. until about noon, after which they would proceed to their private clinics where their income opportunities were greatest. Keep in mind that these officers were already being paid to serve as full-time Army doctors and nurses. Their salaries were almost entirely subsidized by U.S. taxpayer to a level up to twenty times the $400 average annual income for an Afghan household.

It was clear that the "leakage" in the Afghan National Army medical system went far beyond the pilfering of medical supplies. The request to the Department of Defense Inspector General went forward, but it was couched as a request for "assistance" with improving the logistic channels for the ANA's medical supplies.

NATO Training Mission- Afghanistan's Army Development team began meeting regularly after hours to take short-term steps to provide immediate relief to the suffering Afghan patients at the National Military Hospital. Duty hours at Camp Eggers lasted from 8 a.m. to 8 p.m. every day of the week except Fridays, when advisors to the Afghans had a few hours in the morning to themselves while the Afghans marked their day of communal prayer or "Juma." One of my non-commissioned officers proposed a new slogan for the Afghan Government: "The Government of the Islamic Republic of Afghanistan — Rebuilding Afghanistan one half day at a time."

More than once through bleary eyes, someone from the advisory team would comment that the Afghans needed to care about making things better more than we do. Still, we knew we were there to accomplish a mission and do all we could to succeed. If the Afghan mission fails, it won't be because every soldier wearing a Coalition uniform did not give all of his heart and soul, if not life or limb, to the effort.

We took several medical, legal and engineering steps to immediately make things better.

From the medical side, the Medical Training Advisory Group (MTAG) decided to accelerate the residency phase for the military medical students, so they could make rounds and at least provide sanitary conditions for the patients by changing dressings, sheets and providing meals that doctors and nurses had refused.

From the engineering and facilities side, parts to repair heating systems were expedited and installed. Another facilities issue was the need for stable and consistent power from Kabul's grid to run the medical equipment. The National Military Hospital had a generator farm capable of round-the-clock operation, but the fuel for the generators was not secure and was regularly pilfered. U.S. engineers changed the locks on the fuel tanks and ordered an immediate fuel delivery to the National Military Hospital so the generators could begin running 24/7.

On the legal side, we prepared a patients' bill of rights with the Afghan legal and medical folks and a pictorial poster designed to be placed in all areas of all Afghan National Army medical facilities, letting soldiers and family members know what the care and treatment they were entitled to and how to report abuses.

The Afghans mounted mind-numbing counter-measures to our efforts. Many of the medical students failed to show up after they were threatened with violence. Students who arrived to work with Coalition Advisors and Afghan National Army medical trainers found that the doctors and nurses had hidden the patients' charts. The first shipment of fuel never made it to the National Military Hospital. It was stolen by Afghan National Army personnel. The Patients' Bill of Rights posters were ripped off the walls, torn to pieces and thrown to the ground – allegedly "to allow for painting of the walls."

With heavy hearts, we wondered if anything could be done when we cared more than the Afghans did. Many members of the MTAG team were burnt out and deeply disturbed by the inhumanity in which they were immersed. Yet we soldiered on. Eventually, fuel got to the hospital and to our surprise, Karzai, who controls all general officer hiring and firing, agreed to allow the firing of the National Military Hospital Commander and the Afghan National Army Surgeon General. He remained in a paid status while subject to "investigation."

Near the end of 2010, the status of the Afghan National Army medical system was downgraded to CM4 - Red, meaning it was totally dysfunctional. One officer reported that a dismayed General Caldwell described it as "completely broken."

At the end of my tour in March 2011, while waiting for my flight home from Kuwait, I had lunch with a Special Forces advisor who worked with NATO Training Mission - Afghanistan's advisors. He mentioned to me that in 2005 he personally observed the conditions in the National Military Hospital and they were the same then as they were now — brutal and atrocious. With conditions not changing from 2005 to 2010, why did the assessment and public relations reporting show improvement though early 2010?

Could it be that toxic leadership and an eager to please rank and file placed more value on shaping perceptions than recognizing, reporting and addressing realities?

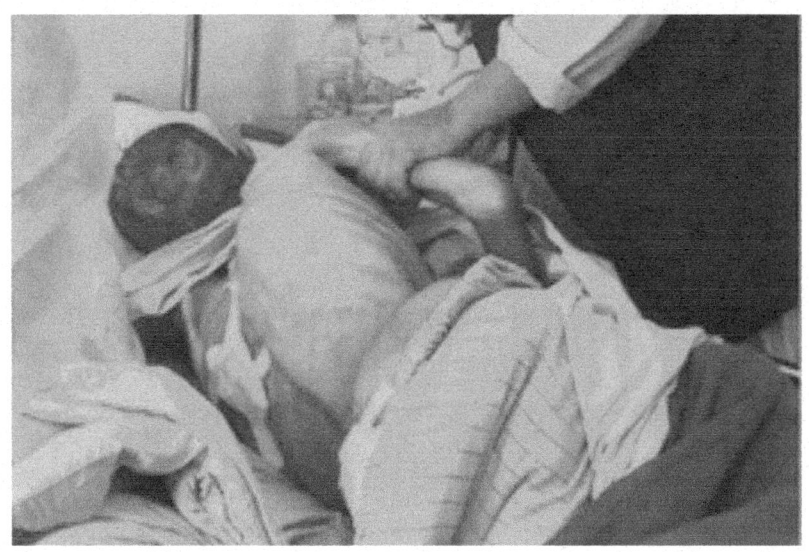

One of many neglected patients at NMH. Photo courtesy of Doctor Schuyler Geller

سرویس عاجل

Me and "Uber JAG" Captain Shane McCammon, U.S. Air Force, with Afghan National Military Hospital and Ministry of Defense Legal Personnel

CHAPTER 12.

THE LORDS OF INDISCIPLINE

"If you do not enforce and maintain discipline, officers
are potential murderers."

General George S. Patton, Jr.[23]

An Afghan National Army convoy moved along a route near Kabul,
with civilians pulling to the right side of the road while flashing their turn
signal to the left. The signal is not used to signify an intent to turn or move
into the left lane, but is a sign of submission to the convoy, indicating that it
may pass to the left. A civilian car moved into the convoy to take advantage
of its swift movement through town. The Afghan National Army soldiers
forced the intruding car and its civilian occupants to the side of the road.[24]
The Afghan soldiers proceeded to beat the senior occupant and then pur-
posefully break his arm. That the soldiers would do this to any civilian

---

23 Peter B. Williamson, Patton's Principals: A Handbook for Managers Who Mean It
(1979) 35.

24 Incident as reported by my Parliamentary Affairs Team.

is troubling enough. That they would do it to a member of Parliament, despite his protests, was a sign of their utter unruliness.

The U.S. Agency for International Development sponsored a 2010 event to promote the rule of law and gender rights among young children. They provided kites with slogans about the law and women. The Afghan National Police came on the scene to "help" with the event. As the excited children pushed their way to the distribution points for the kites, the police began beating the kids over the head with sticks. The police were seen hoarding the kites into their vehicles. When reporters asked them why they were stealing the kites, the police responded that they were not stealing them; they were only using them for themselves.[25]

These are just two examples of the undisciplined nature of the Afghan Security Forces, both Army and Police. There are more examples; to cast these as isolated incidents would be either naïve or disingenuous.

Military justice and the rule of law are critical to building a modern army. George Washington once described discipline as "the soul of an Army." One of his first acts as Commander in Chief of the Continental Army was the appointment of the first Judge Advocate General, a term for a military lawyer — not to review contracts but to help enforce discipline. Washington also petitioned the Continental Congress to increase the number of lashes authorized from 39 to 100. Washington knew that an undisciplined force is a mob that can do more harm than good. Throughout history, disciplined officers have been the ones responsible for keeping their armies in line with the law of armed conflict, a law that is binding on all nations through treaty or international custom.

The implications of an undisciplined force go well beyond the corruption that bleeds our national treasury and undermines the success of our mission in Afghanistan. It can lead to the best equipped, unruly mobs in the history of anarchistic civil war not seen since the 1990s in Afghanistan.

---

25 New York Times, September 24, 2010, "Afghan Equality and Law, but With Strings Attached," by Rod Nordland

After almost a year of working at the top of the Afghan National Army legal chain, my assessment of the Afghan National Army officer corps, which includes officers in the Ministry of Defense, is that they are undisciplined from the top down to the field grade level (majors). Since the American-style military justice system was put in place in 2005, the Afghans, whose country consistently is ranked among the most corrupt in the world, have only prosecuted one sitting general. The Afghans prosecuted the Inspector General for the Ministry of Defense for losing his pistol. Not coincidentally, his prosecution occurred after his effort to investigate the corruption and atrocious conditions at the National Military Hospital. There is no prospect for improvement unless our leadership is prepared to walk away from Afghan leadership. Even then, it may be too late. Only when an Afghan believes that another party is prepared to walk away will he consider changing his behavior.

Some are quick to make excuses for the Afghans and point out that culture complicates the issue. Indeed, when I spoke on this topic at the weekly Senior Advisor dinner at Camp Eggers, the U.S. Army general officers were quick to raise the cultural framework to dismiss the notion that the leadership of the Afghan National Security Forces is undisciplined. Major General Patton confronted me and my immediate commander prior to my presentation, demanding to know whether I would be making generals look bad by "throwing them under the bus."

General Patton gave an example that he claimed demonstrated the complexities of Afghanistan and rendered invalid my "overly simplistic conclusion that the Afghan National Army officers are undisciplined."

A Kandak (Battalion) commander (Lieutenant Colonel) had set up road blocks in his sector and was shaking down travelers for "tolls." The Corps Commander, a two-star general explained to the Afghan Chief of the General Staff, a four-star general, that he could not take action against the Kandak commander because he and the Lieutenant Colonel were from the same village and he could never go home again. The

Corps Commander asked the four-star general to take the disciplinary action. This Corps Commander was not undisciplined; he was asking for help and we needed to be sympathetic to his cultural situation.

I was taken aback by this example because of the thousands of Coalition sons, daughters, brothers, sisters, mothers, and fathers who can never return to their villages because they came to and died in aid of Afghanistan, and the thousands more who have to go home burned or maimed. I found no sympathy for the cowardice expressed by the two-star Afghan general. Worse, the next day I learned that the four-star Afghan general did nothing to that Kandak commander because he was too connected. General Patton's example actually proved my point: The Afghan National Army officer corps is undisciplined from the top down to the field grade level. What other conclusion can one reach when a four-star general is helpless to discipline a connected lieutenant colonel?

No doubt, culture can help explain a great deal about the Afghan security forces we are propping up. However, culture does not excuse the same forces or their Coalition enablers from complying with international laws that bind nations by treaty and custom. The warrior culture of Bushido is thought by some to explain why the Japanese soldiery committed what the world considered atrocities in their treatment of prisoners and civilians, from the Bataan Death March to the wanton death and destruction of Manila. Others will argue that it was the propaganda of a ruthless leadership that bastardized Bushido tenets to bring a poor, uneducated citizenry to wage war ruthlessly. Regardless of the role of Bushido or other cultural frameworks in play, cultural reasons were not defenses in the prosecutions of the Japanese leaders held accountable for the acts of their forces at Bataan and Manila. Some practices, even if culturally based, simply are not compatible with the standards a modern military is bound to follow.

In Afghanistan, the history and culture makes the need for discipline all the more compelling, especially as we equip Afghans with arsenals of modern tools of warfare. Only 15 years ago, the tribes of Afghanistan — the Pashtuns, Tajiks, Hazaras and Uzbeks led by powerful Khans aka warlords — engaged in brutal, continuous and savage warfare among themselves. They brought their country to the brink of the Stone Age by creating the ideal conditions for anarchy and savagery – conditions that made the Taliban's rule of law a welcome force. The Taliban ended the warfare and literally pushed the country backwards in time, but the Afghan people preferred the Taliban's extreme rule of law to the anarchy that preceded it.

Since 2001, when the U.S.-led alliance of Afghan warlords and their militant followers expelled the Taliban from power, officials of the newly formed government have enjoyed impunity. Malign behavior is addressed only after the coalition applies immense pressure. Even then, it is customary for the Afghan leadership to shuffle the perpetrator out of sight until the storm blows over. The bad guy almost always resurfaces later in a position of equal or greater stature. Many of the current senior officers of the Afghan National Army, the Ministry of Defense and the Ministry of the Interior either engaged in or are beholden to the Khans who orchestrated the brutal continuous and savage warfare of the 1990s. Churchill could have been speaking of these same Khans and leaders when he wrote, "The weapons of the nineteenth century are in the hands of the savages of the Stone Age; the strength of civilization without its mercy." The only difference now is that they are armed with the weapons of the 21st century.

In order to understand how the Khans of the 1990s dominate the Afghan National Security Forces, one must understand the Bonn Agreement and Ethnic Balancing.

Ethnic Balancing is a policy supported by the U.S. led coalition, requiring certain percentages of tribes to be maintained throughout the Army. Afghans ranging from the President's General Counsel to four and three-star generals have described Ethnic Balancing as a virus. It is a virus unleashed by the Bonn Agreement, which reestablished the Afghan National Army in December 2002. The agreement was shaped and executed by vicious warlords - Fahim, Sayef, Mohaqiq, Dostom and others - whose hyper-ambition and constant brutal warfare allowed the Taliban to take over Afghanistan in the 1990s. These are men who a high level GIROA official described to me as being as destructive to Afghanistan as the Taliban, just with different approaches. These warlords are, not surprisingly, focused on the Ministries of Defense and Interior – the same institutions that receive $1 billion a month in cash and weaponry from U.S. taxpayers.

Balancing is poisonous and perpetuates the ethnic divisiveness that led to the savagery of the 1990s, keeping things at a slow boil beneath an apparently cooperative facade.

When I met with the Deputy Commander of an Afghan National Army Corps, he said they had no problems with ethnic tensions in his corps. He then rattled off key positions in the corps and the ethnicity of each, unwittingly validating the problem — an emphasis on tribe, not nationality, talent or character. In the U.S., the military led the way out of racism, but the U.S. is promoting a policy that perpetuates it within the Afghan National Army. Ironically, the policy is illegal under Afghan law. The Afghan Constitution prohibits the President, who is the Commander in Chief, from making any decision based on race, tribe, ethnicity or political party. Still, the U.S. promotes ethnic balancing and General Caldwell has stated that the U.S. will continue to do so until President Karzai directs otherwise. Promoting the rule of law to the Afghans is difficult when they see us picking and choosing which laws we wish to see followed and ignoring the constitutional framework of the Afghan system.

According to many educated Afghans with whom I have spoken, including Afghans within and outside of government, the Khans use ethnic balancing as a means of maintaining their share of influence and dominance over the Ministry of Defense and the Afghan National Army. The power and influence of the Khans is so strong that Karzai himself is beholden to them as he tries to keep his government together in the face of the power and relative permanence they yield.[26]

An officer who receives his position through a patron warlord is cloaked in impunity. I once told a prominent high-level general (not within Legal) my belief that ethnic balancing undermines the rule of law in the Ministry of Defense because its sole purpose is a temporary glue that allows the major tribes to steal. Remember, spoils are a means to power in Afghanistan. The general smiled and said, "You are exactly right."

The point was driven home on another occasion, as I sat in the office of the newly appointed Deputy Chief of GS Legal, a general officer position and the number two lawyer in the Afghan National Army. The Deputy was not a lawyer; he was a religious mullah who had managed President Karzai's 2009 re-election campaign in Kabul. Sitting with him were some illiterate mujahideen officers (holy warriors, backed by the CIA in the fight against the Soviets). We talked about the law. They were in a mocking mode, bragging about how they broke the rules in killing many Russians. Then one said to me, "Your generals continue to support our generals who break the law, who don't allow investigations to proceed." They all laughed from the belly. It was not a pleasant moment. They were not laughing at me; they were laughing at my military and my country. It was rather painful.

On more than one occasion when I urged advisees to follow the law, the Afghans were quick to point out the hypocrisy of the Coalition's support of illegal policies. The Coalition is afraid to push the Afghans to follow their own constitution and overcome their racial biases while we are there. Instead, we defer the issue to a point in time in the future. In today's political parlance, we kick the can further down the road.

---

26 For an excellent discussion of Karzai's relationship to the Khans, see "You would cry too: In defense of Hamid Karzai" By Joshua Foust, September 28, 2010. http://afpak.foreignpolicy.com/posts/2010/09/28/ you_would_cry_too_in_defense_of_hamid_karzai)

If arming and fielding a force for Afghanistan is essential to our strategy in Afghanistan, then insisting on discipline from the Ministers of Defense and Interior down to the soldiers in the field is absolutely essential. It must be as non-negotiable as we have made gender issues. Discipline must be enforced from the top down in all that they do, whether in contracting for essential goods and services or relieving officers for dereliction of duty, or arresting and trying murderers and thieves. There is a saying in Afghanistan: "The water runs dirty from the top."

We have an obligation to the world, to our own people, and to the people of Afghanistan not to arm a force with an undisciplined officer corps.

If we cannot break the influence of the Khans and insist on discipline in the Afghan National Army, then it is time for the U.S. to reconsider its policy of giving the Afghans massive amounts of weaponry and money to build that army. The U.S. needs to stop keeping score based on the numbers of boots and bullets. Our roles as advisors, trainers and "correctors" are critical to the discipline needed to build an effective force that won't go berserk on its own people. It extends to the top of the Coalition leadership, both military and civilian, and it must have teeth. Every advisor, every general officer, and every head of state who engages Afghans at every level must insist on the discipline expected of a modern Army. We must be tough, hard-nosed negotiators and be willing to say "no" when it comes time to write the $1 billion per month in Security Assistance checks.

In the Afghan culture, one must demonstrate a willingness to walk away from a deal before an Afghan will come to acceptable terms. Their cultural framework won't allow them to come to such terms until they know we are willing to walk away. Of course, at this late stage, they may indeed let us walk away. If that were to happen, then at least the bleeding of soldiers and the waste of the U.S. Treasury that is borrowing from future generations of Americans will stop sooner, with the Afghan results no worse off now than at the end of 2014, when all combat troops are scheduled to be out.

CHAPTER 13:
LAW AND DISORDER

"First thing we do, let's kill all the lawyers."
Dick the Butcher

There has been some debate on whether Shakespeare's famous line from *Henry the VI* is an anti-lawyer joke or praise for the profession, considering the source. It was probably both. The line is uttered by Dick the Butcher to Jack Cade in a conversation that contemplated a society where they were in complete control, the source of all that their people would want or need. They could have been Afghan Warlords . . . or Afghan corps commanders.

The Afghan National Army's legal system at one time had been the responsibility of the Attorney General's office. In 2005, U.S. legal advisors had worked with the Afghans to draft several laws that changed their system to a self-contained military justice system similar to the U.S. Army. The laws were implemented by Afghan Presidential decree, which is a way to pass laws without Parliament's approval, so long as it is done while

Parliament is in recess. The laws created military courts, military prosecutors, defense counsel, and legal advisors.

Like the U.S. system, the laws placed much of the authority for prosecutions with the military commander. Unlike our system, which preserves the right of the civilian attorney general to prosecute any military member for violations of law, the Afghan system seems to preclude prosecution of military men for any crime that can be prosecuted as a military crime — at least that seems to be the position taken by the officers within the Ministry of Defense and the Afghan National Army.

By building a system in our image, but without any clear authority for the Afghan Attorney General to prosecute generals, the U.S. made a terrible mistake. We vested too much authority in the Commander. Given that all but one of the positions of authority within the Ministry of Defense are occupied by active-duty generals, it is easy to see why no generals have been prosecuted within the Ministry or the Army – except of course for the Inspector General who lost his pistol while probing too deeply into the National Military Hospital scandal.

In our society, where 1% of the population serves in the military, the nuances of military justice are not at the forefront of Americans' concerns. However, the Afghan Ministry of Defense is by far the largest recipient of U.S. tax dollars, raking in the lion's share of the $1 billion we spend each month to build Afghan security forces.

From 2005 to the present, the Afghans established a working military justice system with Coalition assistance. There are courts, detention facilities, prosecutors, defense counsel and legal advisors throughout all of the military corps. Lawyers fill more than 90 percent of judicial positions. There were and continue to be a regular docket of court martial prosecutions.

But only junior soldiers are prosecuted, usually only for crimes such as vehicular homicide, petty theft, and losing weapons. A typical case I observed in the town of Mez a Sharif at the 209th Corps, involved the prosecution of a junior enlisted soldier for vehicular manslaughter and damage to property. The soldier, like most Afghan soldiers, drove recklessly, killing a young girl and damaging the army vehicle. The court disposed of the easy count first. The defense attorney presented a letter from the dead girl's father explaining that he was satisfied with the defendant's apology and the cooking oil and rice he provided to the family as reparation. The more difficult part of the trial revolved around the issue of damage to the vehicle and how much the soldier would have to repay to his commander.

The corps commanders treat their corps as their franchise. Each corps is static, meaning it sits in one section of Afghanistan and is responsible for that sector's "security." If word of a crime surfaces involving an officer or member of a tribe or patronage network, the corps commander would typically have his intelligence officer investigate to determine whether his interests were impacted by the matter. In cases where the legal officer learned of the incident, the corps commander would typically put pressure on the senior corps legal advisor to ignore the matter and would deny vehicles and other resources to legal personnel.

It often worked, but not always. Occasionally, a motivated legal officer, typically from the younger genre, would leak word of the incident to the Coalition corps legal trainers who would relay the information to Kabul. The Chief of GS Legal would sometimes be able compel a prosecution.

Some tactical successes in establishing the rule of law included the prosecution and conviction of an Afghan soldier who murdered U.S. Army Staff Sergeant Anthony Spino near Herat in December 2009. When word got to Kabul of a prosecutor fixing the trial for an acquittal, the Chief of GS Legal fired him and replaced him with another. The Afghan soldier was convicted on testimony of Americans, Italians and most importantly, Afghans. The court sentenced him to death.

The December 2009 media reports on the death of Staff Sergeant Spino stated he had been killed by an insurgent. The trial ensured that justice had been served, advancing the rule of law. The local Public Affairs

Office prepared a press release. I saw it forwarded to Washington, but the PAO command here declined to release the news to the press.

Another tactical success came when an Uzbek kandak (battalion) commander, who had a previous conviction for raping several of his male subordinates, was accused of attempted rape of the wife of a subordinate. The commander went AWOL to visit his Uzbek protectors in Kabul. But a coordinated effort between the Afghan Inspector General and the Chief of GS Legal and their respective Coalition advisors stopped an effort by the Dostom led Uzbek community to quash the investigation. A prosecution ensued. Unfortunately, prior to trial, legal counsel for the rapist commander produced a signed retraction from the victim and her husband, asking that the charges be dropped. The couple disappeared. While the court was unable or unwilling to convict the rapist commander with the retraction, the court did convict him of abuse of authority for breaking into the couple's home. He was sentenced to six months confinement and removed from command. Shortly before the end of my tour, the Afghan leadership put him back in command of his kandak. When word got out that the rapist was back in command, an embarrassed Afghan leadership removed him — at least for the time being.

Another success that started before I left involved an Afghan Commando unit, supposedly the type of Afghan unit that can actually perform some traditional military tasks. The unit had an unusually low rate of AWOL. It turned out that some of the Afghans had twisted direct deposit, one of our anti-fraud measures, into a cash cow. Until 2009, most commanders had siphoned off the cash payroll made to unit members. Direct deposit was a way to boost morale by giving all soldiers a raise in the form of 100% of their actual pay.

But, at 209th Corps, a finance officer and personnel officer realized that if they did not report soldiers as AWOL, they could divert the soldiers' pay to a private account and split the booty. The court martial convicted the officers, two majors who were just below the generally connected level of colonels.

More common were stories of corps commanders summarily throwing people in detention facilities or ordering their comrades released without proper authority. In one case, after an Afghan legal officer determined that a soldier in temporary detention was entitled to be released, the corps commander had the legal officer arrested and thrown into the same facility. In the case of the rapist kandak commander, members of the corps commander's staff threatened the legal advisor and his family with bodily harm after he refused to order the release of the convict. While acts like this were reported almost daily to the Coalition chain of command, they were nuisance issues, not worthy of discussion with the Minister of Defense.

The Minister was always more concerned about lifting the ceiling on the size of the Afghan National Army and the consequent funding from the U.S. taxpayer that would come from having a larger Army. From the Afghans' perspective, the Minister controlled whether any prosecutorial investigation would be allowed against an officer of rank. That is not how the laws read, but that was the de facto law of the current Ministry of Defense. The Minister clearly had the influence to say no to an effective investigation, but given the warlord politics of Afghanistan, I doubt he had authority to say yes. The same can be said of President Karzai.

Despite the near impossible obstacles to implementing the rule of law in Afghanistan, my team did what we could to at least keep building a disciplined framework of laws. Whether the Afghans will ever allow it to work remains to be seen.

Before returning home, my team worked with the Afghans to completely reorganize the Afghan Army's military justice system. The corps legal offices were broken away from the corps commanders, making them independent and more like the Canadian military, but more importantly, something the Afghan legal officers wanted. An army legal school was started with a team of advisors and the construction of a $12 million facility. A bit rich, the plans and funding for the school had been in place for a few years. Thirty two law graduates were commissioned as legal officers, representing the greatest hope for the military rule of law.

The down side of that story was the loss of 34 law graduates because of delays in commissioning due to disputes over ethnic balancing. The Afghans drafted and "implemented" decrees that defined and prohibited conflicts of interest among the lawyers, required officers in legal positions to be lawyers and mandated strict compliance with record keeping and subpoenas. Was it "measured progress," or just another round of Buzkashi so the latest group of Coalition advisors would keep the money flowing?

ANA Private Saleh Muhammed, left, receiving his death sentence for shooting and killing U.S. Army Staff Sergeant Ronald Spino who was unloading medical supplies from a helicopter near Herat.

Brigadier General Gary Patton presents a commander's coin for the role my team played in removing a corrupt prosecutor, clearing the way for a fair trial of an Afghan Soldier who murdered U.S. Army Staff Sergeant Ronald Spino.

Uniformed defense counsel and an Afghan soldier accused of vehicular manslaughter of a young girl stand before a court-martial at 209th Corps in Mez a Sharif.

CHAPTER 14:
HOMEWARD BOUND

"Having now finished the work assigned to me, I retire
from the great theatre of Action."

George Washington, December 23, 1783.

As the end date of a tour approaches, fatigue abounds — physical, mental and spiritual. Closing your eyes can be difficult. Visions of home become so vivid that you need to remind yourself you are not home yet, and that you need to be vigilant in your mission and alert to your surroundings.

Working on a "continuity turnover binder" brings together a year's worth of efforts, accomplishments, shortfalls, celebrations and disappointments. The binder represents a ticket home, an attempt at continuity as the next in a long line of short-term advisors arrives to deal with the Afghan leadership. With the binder comes farewell ceremonies and meals, parting gifts and the opportunity to reflect.

The greatest problem facing Afghanistan is common to many parts of the world — the unwillingness to give up power. To the Afghans, rank is power and power is survival. General Petraeus said in his corruption and transparency briefing early in his tour that the key for Afghanistan would be for those with the power to let go enough so that institutions based on the rule of law could take hold. In other words, Afghanistan would need to be blessed with a George Washington, a man whose willingness to step away from power made the United States the fruitful nation that I will never take for granted.

My tour was spent looking for George Washington and if he is there, he is hidden well. More likely, he or she is probably not much older than 25. My parting gift to Major General Nooristani was a portrait of General George Washington resigning his military commission to the Continental Congress in 1783 and his speech translated to Dari. At my urging, the Army Development team suggested to Defense Minister Rahim Wardak, who retained the active rank of four-star general, that he retire from his rank and serve the duration of his time as a purely civilian minister. The suggestion went unheeded by the Minister.

Looking back on the year of the surge, a compelling measuring stick was discouraging — the lack of freedom of movement. Despite the flow of billions of dollars of equipment, goods, construction and money into the coffers of the Government of the Islamic Republic of Afghanistan, more territory seemed to be considered unsafe or trending in that direction. Officers arriving for their second or third tour commented how surprised they were at the constraints on movements due to hostile or perceived hostile environments. Maps used by Non-Government Organizations (NGOs) and the UN as guides for areas of safe transport showed dramatically less territory, including areas in the north once considered fiercely anti-Taliban. In the summer of 2010, a Taliban orchestrated stoning of a young couple in Kunduz province made world news because of its brutality and because of its location in the north.

The lack of discipline in the Afghan Security Forces from top down surfaced in a variety of ways, including AWOL rates and the medical system rating. The near collapse of the country's banking system showed little hope for financial discipline. The incidents of uniformed Afghans turning their weapons on U.S. and other Coalition troops, known as "Green on Blue," began to pick up as the year wore on. Some were reported in the press as Green on Blue and some were reported as "killed in combat operations." More often in Kabul, insurgents have been able to pass through numerous checkpoints unchecked to get into the Ministry of Defense, the Green Zone near the U.S. Embassy and the National Military Hospital to carry out attacks. Those attacks indicate enemy infiltration of the Afghan Security Forces or the shifting of allegiances among their members, a phenomenon that is historically very Afghan.

What is going right? Where is the hope for success?

Ironically, the answer is counter-terrorism, which is what Vice President Joe Biden argued should have been the U.S. focus and strategy in lieu of a surge of troops and money for counter-insurgency.

When General Petraeus took over in July of 2010, he dramatically increased the number of night raids similar to the one that killed Bin Laden, although not as rehearsed. Every night numerous missions were flown capturing or killing leaders of the Taliban and Al Qaeda in Afghanistan and on the Pakistan border. The U.S.-led Coalition has been killing and capturing insurgent leaders by the bushel.

Regarding counter-insurgency, Major General Nooristani would insist that the U.S. needs to think of South Korea as the model for its approach in Afghanistan — a fifty year commitment that outlasted the massive corruption there and resulted in a stable government and solid economy.

There is some merit to the argument. There are some young Afghans who might grow to become the kind of leaders that can see beyond their own power and survival and agree to work toward a civic good. Leaders like the lieutenant who told the truth about the murder of the twelve-year-old girl near Herat by Afghan soldiers or the lieutenant who blew the whistle on his corps commander for beating and jailing a staff officer.

For the fifty-year generational model to work, the Afghan people would have to let us stay in their country for fifty years. The Afghan people don't have a good track record of allowing foreigners to remain in their land for long periods and they seemed to be already tiring of our presence. Also, the American people would have to agree to a 50 year commitment and they barely seem interested in the commitment to 2014.

There were reports of Afghan generals doing cartwheels when they learned of the Republican sweep in the 2010 Congressional elections, believing that the results would keep the American military and treasury committed to Afghanistan beyond our Democratic president's deadline of 2014. I explained how the elections of November 2010 were dramatic in the number of Republican victories, but that those victories said nothing of U.S. policy toward Afghanistan. Afghanistan was never discussed in the campaigns leading up to the 2010 election. The big discussion was over tea parties and how the U.S. needed to stop spending so much money — a discussion that would do well to focus on the money spent on our efforts in Afghanistan.

So where do we go from here? No serious person who knows the ground truth in Afghanistan expects any real change to take hold by 2014.

There are serious folks who have the facts on the ground vetted for them by an eager-to-please staff, but they are lacking in ground truth. The Afghans benefiting from their corruption have been trained by us to know that the money will keep flowing because of our fear of failure — no matter how much they siphon away or how poorly they behave. It would be as hard to change our complicit, check-writing behavior as it would to change the corrupt, blind-eye behavior of the Afghan leadership.

Do we stay until 2014 to try and save face and hope it doesn't crumble until 2015? There is a cost in terms of money and lives — those lost and those changed forever by physical and emotional wounds. Or do we commit to the fifty-year generational model of change? U.S. civilian leadership has not been talking about these choices in a candid manner. As I write these words, Mitt Romney, the leading contender for the Republican presidential nomination said he has no plan for Afghanistan. If elected president of the United States, a nation currently at war in Afghanistan, he has said he will have experts brief him on the situation and then come up with a plan. It hurts my heart to no end that war has become an afterthought to our civilian leaders.

I served in Afghanistan with brothers and sisters, sons and daughters who make up the 1% of our population who served our Nation in time of war. The Afghan War seemed to become a forgotten war, an afterthought, just months after it started in October 2001. Yet it is the longest war in our nation's history — three times longer than World War II, two-and-a-half times longer than our bloody civil war and even longer than the Vietnam conflict. The 99% who do not serve our nation in time of war can best honor the 1% by learning of their fight and never forgetting.

No war should be on automatic pilot, an afterthought of the American people. Every person has to be passionate about war. It is something that must be done right or not done at all. Everyone is morally duty bound to know what is going on and, if convinced of the righteousness of the cause, assure that all is given to achieve victory as quickly as possible. And if the cause appears to be folly, a waste of our precious resource, then push our leadership to preserve that resource, those boys and girls, and bring them home. Learn, act and remember. That is how we honor our veterans.

As we consider the effectiveness of our counter-insurgency efforts in Afghanistan and contemplate the way forward, some words from Winston Churchill written in 1897 about one of Britain's three failed efforts in Afghanistan seem timely today:

Military rule is the rule best suited to the character and com-prehension of the tribesmen. They will soon recognize the futility of resistance, and will gradually welcome the increase of wealth and comfort that will follow a stable government...

Only one real objection has been advanced against this plan. But it is a crushing one, and it constitutes the most serious argument against the whole "Forward Policy." It is this: we have neither the troops nor the money to carry it out. . . . The reproach which may be justly laid upon the British rulers . . . whether at home or abroad, is that while they recognize the facts, they shrink from the legitimate conclusions. . . .They know they cannot turn back. They fully intend to go on. Yet they fear to admit the situation, to frankly lay their case before the country, and trust to the good sense and courage of an ancient democracy.

Winston Churchill

Carl Von Clausewitz, the father of modern strategy, said, "Two qualities (of leadership) are indispensable: first, an intellect that, even in the darkest hour, retains some glimmerings of the inner light which leads to the truth; and second, the courage to follow that light wherever it may lead."

The harsh reality is that the only way the U.S. is going to successfully build an Afghan military that can function as a pillar of a legitimate, stable Afghan government, is if the U.S. is willing to walk away from Afghan leaders who refuse to change their behavior.

It may, in fact, be too late, and we have to be prepared for them to show us the door. However, if we continue our timid approach of the dot-ing parent who can't say no to the spoiled Afghan Government officials, they will continue to use our resources to advance their own short-sighted, alienating behavior. They will perpetuate a culture of warlords that has kept Afghanistan as one of the most backward and strangest of places on Earth.

Only when you demonstrate that you are truly ready to walk away from the table, do you stand a chance that an Afghan will reach out to you to make the deal you want and then say to you "are you happy my friend?"

Presenting Major General Nooristani with a painting of George Washington surrendering his military commission to the Continental Congress in 1783 as Brigadier General Abdul Karim, senior uniformed lawyer looks on.

CHAPTER 15

THE SOCIAL SIDE OF WAR

"Friendship improves happiness, and abates misery, by doubling our joys, and dividing our grief."

👍 **Joseph Addison likes this.**

One percent of the population knows firsthand the many forms of pains of war. All know of the grief of lost loved ones and the pain borne by youth maimed, although few are at risk of experiencing it. The 99% who don't serve our nation often don't appreciate the lesser but more frequent sacrifices of the 1%. The loneliness of long deployments, the anxiety felt on both ends of the world by the soldier worried for his loved ones at home and the loved ones agonizing each time they hear news of the war. Some miss the birth of a child, their first steps, or the first poopy in the potty — moments stolen and never recouped.

There is the anguish of not being there for loved ones who experience the pain of growing up or worse trauma that might find them. Other soldiers, try as they might, get home too late to say good-bye to a loved one who succumbs to illness. Affections become alienated and families tear apart in a never-ending deployment cycle of one year on and one year "off" preparing for the next. Through it all, family and friendships can make impossible situations more bearable.

The Department of Defense's decision to embrace social networking sites has been a tremendous boost to morale. One of the great blessings for soldiers downrange has been communications technology, including Skype and Facebook. In addition to the obvious capability of keeping in touch with loved ones on a frequent basis, social networking technology, especially Facebook, helps connect the 1% with the 99%.

Throughout my tour, I was able to keep my family and friends informed of life in a war zone from mundane cravings, like missing fresh ground pepper, to more complex challenges, like explaining American civics to the Afghan leadership. Of course, when you post that you miss any item, it appears in mail within days, unless it violates General Order One. And getting stuff in the mail is one of the few joys in theater.

Not all social engagement is through computers. The friendships made in military service are deep and lifelong. Spending long hours in an intense environment brings a range of emotions. Fiery disputes and rivalries can evolve into deep respect and admiration and the reverse can happen, although usually temporarily. Some of the darkest moments came when arguments, fierce and too personal, would break out amongst teammates. That's to be expected when so much is on the line — storming then norming.

The stress of frequent and long deployments has taken a dark toll on our precious, all-volunteer force. That dark tragedy is the rate of suicide, which, as mentioned previously, has set a new record every year since 2008. The Army and its chaplains have made a concerted effort to raise awareness of suicide among soldiers. Signs of the awareness were evident throughout my tour. From a soldier who gave testimony at a church service in Camp Spann of his near suicide, to a friend who had his weapon taken after losing his family to the alienation of long multiple separations.

Always, there was an understanding of the problem with no negative judgment. And through it all, the chaplains, gifts from God, were always there to comfort the pain and helplessness that can breed on a lonely forward operating base.

For the 99% who read this book and wish to engage, please do connect with the 1%. Ask them how they are doing and what they did. Do send them stuff: cards, coffee, movies, cigars, body wash (perfumed for the women soldiers) and more. The appreciation is real. More importantly, if you see a wounded warrior, ask them how it happened. He or she has a story to tell and they want to share it. Divide their grief and increase their joy.

One of the best things you can do to honor the 1% who serve is to stay informed and passionate about what they do. Take a stand. There is no resource more precious than a nation's children who serve at its beckon. We all must be stewards of that resource.

Enjoying near beer and some laughs. Thanksgiving 2010. Colonel Doug Seagraves, USAF; Colonel Malcolm Bruce, CAN; Brigadier General David Neasmith, CAN.

Colonel Mike Kawaguchi, U.S. Marine Corps; Colonel Dave Daniels, Utah Army National Guard; Steve Dade, Senior Executive Service and U.S. Marine Corps (Retired)

EPILOGUE

"I tell you, on the day of judgment people will give
account for every careless word they speak, for by your
words you will be justified, and by your words you
will be condemned."

Matthew 12:36-37

It's been almost two years since my return from "the Stan," three years since the surreal trek to that strange place began. For some time, "How are things going" was an uncomfortable question, and many were afraid to ask. Transition to normal life was much harder than expected. "War is Hell." General Sherman's quote is cliché to many, but solemn truth to those who experience it - including families.

If war is hell, then coming home can be a purgatory, where relationships fray from simmering resentment borne of separation, stress and other traumas of life. Some can be mended, others will never be the same. War does not just happen to soldiers, it happens to their families. Family trauma is not mine alone and the details must remain private out of respect for my loved ones who also bear the scars of war. For many of the warriors who fought our Nation's wars, they continue to fight the demons of war that can linger, whether physical, mental or spiritual.

For months, panic would disrupt sleep at 3 a.m. without a clue why. It made no sense when sleep seemed easy and reliable to come by in Afghanistan. Perhaps the numbing mechanism essential to survival and the courage necessary to function in such an environment has a lingering counter effect once home. Complaints of co-workers and bosses seemed trivial and made for a short temper. Things may not be going as planned, but people aren't dying. Get over it. For me it passed, but one thing lingered: the frustration of having been close to an insane effort that cost money and lives, was certain to fail by every sober metric, and seemed forgotten at home. Almost daily there were reports of precious lives lost and a rise in reporting of "Green on Blue" murders - the killing of American and other allied soldiers by uniformed Afghans. It was always on our minds in Afghanistan, not at all rare - and not always reported.

In late April of 2011 came a most gruesome news report: a "mentally ill" Afghan Colonel "acting alone" with a pistol murdered nine armed U.S. Air Force advisors to the Afghan Army Air Force. The short hair on the back of my neck stood up and my heart raced. The email chatter amongst my advisor brothers was furious that day, but was comforting. Chopper Slook, naval aviator and fellow senior advisor to the Afghan Army Air Force, was safe. Power Point may have saved his life. That morning, he decided to stay put at Camp Eggers and work on a briefing for the command instead of attending the fateful meeting with the Afghan Colonel. Stories were later published about the U.S. funded Afghan Air Force smuggling drugs and guns and engaging in other illegal activities under U.S. noses. The murdered advisors were reportedly confronting the Afghans about the illicit activity at the time of their demise. Of course, the official website for NTM-A would report none of it. Mystery flights by the

Afghan Air Force were characterized as "neglect of proper maintenance at recommended intervals."

This book started as a form of therapy. At first, it was cautious, borne of concern that the raw truth would draw scorn and controversy - something no career officer wants. However, that watered down elixir was ineffective. Only when the truth rolled off my fingertips onto the backlit keys of my MacBook did the medicine take effect. All medicine has side effects, some good, some bad.

During the advisory mission, many of the advisors on the Army team (those training the Afghan Army) developed close relationships, fostered in large part by the team spirit instilled by its leader, Canadian Brigadier General David Neasmith. We spoke often of the challenges facing Afghanistan, foremost being the cancerous corruption, allowed to fester unchecked by an autocratic government funded and empowered by misguided U.S. largesse. In one memorable conversation, I spoke of the checks and balances of a stable three-legged stool that is a government with an effective legislature, independent court system and an executive. Afghanistan was missing two of those legs. Fellow advisor Colonel Bill Brei, U.S. Air Force reminded me of the fourth leg that strengthens the people's hold on government: a free press.

My reporting in Afghanistan was always straight and unfiltered by the rose-colored glasses that have become standard issue for too many general officers and their hand-picked like-minded, career-myopic staff officers. While I was serving, many civilians and fellow officers were drawn to my daily reports and regularly complimented me for "telling it like it is," including my one time senior rater and General Caldwell's civilian deputy, Dr. Jackie Kem. When it was my turn to give my farewell speech at the senior advisor's dinner, attendance swelled, bringing in many advisors who had stopped coming to what they perceived to be a Kool-Aid festival. The large crowd prompted Major General Gary S. Patton to confront me and my boss, Brigadier General David Neasmith, warning both of us that I better not make generals look bad by throwing them under the bus.

A reporter from the *Wall Street Journal*, Maria Abi-Habib got wind of the dysfunction that was the Dawoo National Military Hospital and the leadership of the NATO Training Mission - Afghanistan. My name came to her attention, as did an email exchange between General Caldwell and me. Her call came as I was about two-thirds through this book. I spoke to her, albeit reluctantly and carefully.

My greatest concern in speaking with a reporter, more than the effect it might have on my career which was in its twilight, was that I not be part of a slanted swipe at my brothers and sisters in uniform who gave so much to make things work and to reduce human suffering. The horrid conditions at the hospital were not symptoms of U.S. and coalition soldiers losing touch with their humanity, as may have been the case with Abu Ghraib, an infamous U.S. run prison in Iraq. The hospital was a symptom of folly borne of a callous Afghan leadership with seemingly unconditional support from a U.S. military leadership eager to keep their eyes plausibly blind, rather than undermine their public message of success and their quest for a punched ticket to a promotion. I spoke candidly with Maria about the situation and expressed my concern with how the *Wall Street Journal* might present the story. I was not willing to go on the record, meaning to be openly quoted, unless I could see the final draft of the article before it went to press. My request was contrary to the paper's long-standing policy, so I declined to go on the record.

The story went to press on September 3, 2011, but without the allegations regarding the command's effort to stop, then narrow the scope of a requested investigation. To report it, the paper needed a minimum number of off-the-record confirmations of what happened or an on-the-record testimonial. The story still had a strong impact, resulting in an immediate demand by House Representative Michael Coffman, a Marine officer, for a Congressional investigation into the U.S. Mission as it related to the funding and support for the Afghan hospital. Representative Jason Chaffetz (R

- Utah), Chairman of the National Security Subcommittee on Oversight and Government Reform, opened such an inquiry into the issue. The Chairman made demands on the Secretary of Defense for documentation and other evidence, including by name requests for me and Colonel Mark Fassl to testify before the committee regarding the support to the Afghan Army hospital, the pilfering of such support, and the circumstances regarding efforts to bring in outside investigators to look into the fraud, waste and abuse that took place at NATO Training Mission - Afghanistan. I received a call from Representative Chaffetz and the counsel to the committee who requested I come to Washington to give testimony of what I saw, did and experienced during my tour.

When it came time to testify, I brought my daughter with me to Washington, D.C. The day before the hearing, I took her to the Holocaust Museum. We stood outside the museum on a bright sunny July day. My daughter had been there before, but I wanted to see it with her. Fresh off a tour of the Capitol Building, we walked the halls of the museum and took in the horror and heroics of humanity. As we finished our visit to the museum, we walked through the Hall of Remembrance where a quote from the bible caught my eye:

> Only guard yourself and guard your soul carefully, lest you
> forget the things your eyes saw, and lest these things depart
> your heart all the days of your life, and you shall make them
> known to your children, and to your children's children.
> Deuteronomy 4:9

The next day I would stand with three of my brothers and raise my hand before Congress to give oral testimony on events in Afghanistan. Earlier in the week, per protocol, I had submitted a written statement. Like much of my writing, the statement flowed freely from my head through my fingers as they tapped my MacBook keys. One reference slipped my mind completely until the next day.

At 9:55 a.m., full of coffee and taking in the scene of a richly appointed room with bright lights and leather chairs, I stood between Colonel Fassl and Colonel Doc Geller, with Captain Andersen to the left. The chairman picked up his gavel and as it swung downward, Colonel Fassl, standing tall in his blue Army uniform, looked over to me and said "well, here we are." My retirement from the Army only days old, wearing a suit and tie, I raised my right hand and swore before God to tell the truth, the whole truth and nothing but the truth. And I did. We all did.

The Chairman gave his opening statement and right out of the box, he mentioned my name and quoted me describing conditions at the Afghan National Military Hospital as "Auschwitz like." My heart skipped a beat - I had forgotten the reference. The quote would appear on CNN and in print media all over the globe that day. There were critical comments by some who were offended by the reference because the hospital was one of neglect, not systemic isolation and extermination that placed Auschwitz in the sub-basement of human experience. For me, the trauma of seeing the videos and photos of the Nazi camps, burned into my young brain the ghostly images of living skeletons with dark sunken eyes. Slow death from starvation seemed as cruel as man could get. The images from the Afghan National Military Hospital struck that synapse in me which led to the reference - Auschwitz like. Not ashamed of the reference, I am sensitive to those who did not appreciate it.

A career officer does not aspire to testifying before Congress, especially to speak ill of senior leadership. There was concern among us about attacks by whichever party felt threatened by our testimony. The bipartisan discussion that took place amongst the Democrats and Republicans was surprising and welcomed. Representative Chaffetz (Republican), chairman of the subcommittee, said

> This has perhaps been the most honest and unvarnished assessment of Afghanistan that Congress has ever had. I

cannot imagine you being more forthright and more candid than the five gentlemen sitting on this panel. I thank you for that.[27]

Representative Tierney (Democrat) commented:

Mr. Chairman, I don't know if you want to go to the full Committee or stay within the confines of the Subcommittee but I think we have to look at the structure. What is missing when obviously the investments we are making in terms of policy, money and personnel and not getting the results that are sought, why we don't have mechanisms for reports to call attention to this and to be acted upon on that basis. We have not just specific instances of a contract that wasn't properly written but of a policy that has gone awry when people complain about the system, violations or problems within it, no way to compel action on that. The attitude seems to be I am not going to rock that boat, I am just a general here for whatever time I am here for, a colonel or whatever, all the way down the line. I am just going to get in here and get out and I don't want all the problems of policy associated with that. Somehow, we have to try to find out where that has gone awry and move forward to see whether or not something like the contingency Inspector General is part of the solution or all of the solution. I suspect that is not all of the solution but where we might go from there.

I want to thank all of you again for your testimony. It was certainly courageous of you to come forward. I think it is what we expect of our military but on the other hand, we don't always see it. We appreciate the frankness and the willingness to come forward. I know it is a difficult thing for you to do but

27 DAWOOD NATIONAL MILITARY HOSPITAL AFGHANISTAN: WHAT HAPPENED AND WHAT WENT WRONG? https://www.govinfo.gov/content/pkg/CHRG-112hhrg75522/pdf/CHRG-112hhrg75522.pdf at page 68.

we appreciate it. I am hoping we can work with the Chairman to do something about it.[28]

In the weeks that followed, word came back from an instructor at the Command and General Staff College at Fort Leavenworth that the testimony had invigorated his class of young Army majors who had become disillusioned with the meek or self-absorbed senior leaders. The professor commented to Colonel Fassl that we had "saved the officer corps." I recalled having a drink earlier that year with a major who served with me in the reserve. He had served in Afghanistan several years earlier and had bemoaned to me

> "sir, for years I have been taught about the virtues of Army values and the great leadership that sets our military apart from other militaries around the world and institutions within our country. Then I served in Afghanistan and I wonder, Sir, where is that leadership?"

Hopefully, officers like him won't lose faith and serve on and become and mentor the officers that our Nation needs.

The Department of Defense Inspector General reached out to me and others who testified before Congress. After interviewing each of us, they encouraged us to file complaints of restriction and retaliation. Military investigations are almost always done by line officers, meaning officers who serve on the lines in command and support functions. Rarely are they done by professionals who have made a career of making lines of questioning designed to lead to meaningful disclosure of information from subjects who are reluctant to discuss uncomfortable topics or who are downright deceptive. There is also a presumption of regularity within the military. It can be a high burden to overcome this presumption, especially when dealing with the highest levels of leadership and especially when those leaders wear the ring of the U.S. Military Academy. All of that said, in the end, the arrogance of Lieutenant General Caldwell, and the weak

---

28 Id. at pg. 66-67.

spine of Major General Gary Patton, lead to an adverse finding by the DoD IG against both.

According to reports of the investigation, General Caldwell issued written orders by email that no one in his command, especially his IG and Command Surgeon, divulge any information without his approval to the DoD IG team on its way to Afghanistan to investigate the Afghan National Military Hospital situation. He asked General Patton to enforce this order in his absence. General Patton, instead of challenging his commander on this illegal order, an obligation of every officer, instead reinforced it, passing it on to others. The DoD IG recommended that the Secretary of the Army take appropriate action against the two officers. To many of those who served under both officers in Afghanistan, this adverse finding came as no surprise. Despite rebuttals by both officers, their stupidity in writing left no room for the DoD-IG to make any other conclusion as much as some in leadership may have wanted.

In a letter dated November 8, 2013 by the Secretary of the Army to Senator Chuck Grassley (Republican - Iowa), a champion of whistleblower rights and communications, the Secretary advised that Secretary Hagel decided to allow Caldwell to retire at his current rank. "The DoD IG's findings have directly influenced this outstanding officer's decision to leave the Army. As you may know, he had great potential to advance to General. . . . The incident in question directly resulted in the termination of his career." In December of 2013, Secretary Hagel announced he was replacing Major General Gary S. Patton from his position as chief of the Pentagon's Task Force on Sexual Assault Prevention, an issue President Obama had declared to be of the highest priority and that the general would be retiring in the Spring. General Patton denied that the DoD IG negative findings had anything to do with his removal or decision to retire.

Meanwhile, the war continues with rosy assessments from the top such as the departing General Allen who replaced General Petraeus as Commander of International Security Assistance Force. On the ground, reports from the rank and file confirm the assessment you have read here. A presidential election came and went in 2012 with Afghanistan hardly mentioned, even in the presidential debate devoted to foreign policy! When it did come up, then presidential Republican nominee Mitt Romney started his commentary by saying

> [t]he surge (in Afghanistan) has been successful, and the training program is proceeding at pace. There are now a large number of Afghan security forces, 350,000, that are — are ready to step in to provide security. And — and we're going to be able to make that transition by the end of — of 2014. So our troops'll come home at that point.

Not surprisingly, President Obama made similar comments touting the "successes" of his Afghanistan strategy. Neither side wanted to shed light on or deal with the folly that was and is Afghanistan.

The only bright spot seems to be the Obama administration's commitment to end the operation in 2014. There is some tepid discussion about the shape and extent of the U.S. presence after 2014, however this author sees no desire on the part of the Obama administration or Congress to make any serious commitment beyond 2014. All sides except for Senators John McCain and Lindsey Graham seem to sheepishly understand the pathetic waste that has been Operation Enduring Freedom. None can do better than let the clock run out. In the meantime, another quarter of a trillion dollars will be wasted between now and the end of 2014. Worse, more sons, daughters, fathers and mothers will die or be maimed as our Nation's leadership stands to the side with their hands behind their backs. The situation begs the question asked by now Secretary of State John Kerry: "How do you ask a man to be the last man to die for a mistake?" How indeed.

There is a light at the end of the tunnel. The war in Afghanistan will come to a wholly unsatisfying end and healing at the macro and micro level will start in earnest. At the macro level, there will be national reflection on both the Iraqi and Afghan wars: how they were started; how they were executed; how they were funded; how they were manned; how they were reported; how defense contractor funded think tanks influenced civilian and military leaders and courses of action; and which companies profited from the courses of actions promoted by the think tanks. The military will reflect on and debate the quality of leadership needed to succeed verse the leadership displayed and, we hope, will take the right steps to close the gap for our Nation's future success. Equally important will come the micro healing, where veterans and their loved ones seek and find inner peace and joy in their lives. For this veteran, that joy comes in the form of a first grandson. For in a baby, hope springs eternal.

In the Capitol Building before the painting of Washington surrendering his military commission to the Continental Congress

Colonel Mark Fassl, U.S. Army, Colonel Schuyler Geller, U.S. Air Force, Colonel Jerry Carozza, U.S. Army and Captain Steve Andersen, U.S. Coast Guard.

GLOSSARY

5001	An Afghan foundational regulatory scheme that establishes the structure and roles for command and control of the Afghan Army and Air Force.
101st Airborne Division	An Army division that calls Fort Campbell, Kentucky home, the 101st Airborne first saw action on D-Day jumping into Normandy and its E Company was featured in the book and television series "Band of Brothers."
10th Mountain Division	A light infantry division that calls Fort Drum, New York home. In World War II, this unit had ski borne soldiers trained to fight in the Alps of Europe. After World War II, veterans of the 10th Mountain Division started the U.S. Ski industry by opening ski resorts throughout the country.

10th SFG(A) - The Tenth Special Forces Group (Airborne).	A Special Forces Group is a unit equal in status to an Army Division, although much smaller in size, that focuses on a region of the world. The 10th SFG(A) focuses on Europe and Southwest Asia.
1st MEF - First Marine Expeditionary Force	A large force made up of a Marine Division of ground forces, a Marine Wing that is a mini air force and other specialized ground units made up of Marines. The 1st MEF is headquartered in Camp Pendleton, California.
AfPak - Afghanistan Pakistan	A term used to describe the Afghanistan Pakistan region.
ANA - Afghan National Army	The largest of the Afghan Security Forces paid for by the U.S.
ANP - Afghan National Police	An Afghan Security Force, the ANP are a paramilitary police force.
Apache	A heavily armed attack helicopter used by the U.S. Army designed to kill tanks and fortified positions.
Army Ranger or Tabbed Ranger	Soldiers trained in enhanced land navigation and small unit tactics, they deploy by land sea and air. They undergo a 6-week course at Fort Benning to become Ranger qualified. Rangers wear a tab on their left shoulder that reads "RANGERS" and are sometimes referred to as "Tabbed Rangers."
AWOL - Absent Without Leave	A term used to describe military members who are absent from their place of duty without permission. AWOL is a crime.

BBC - British Broadcasting Company	Television and Radio broadcasting from the U.K.
C&GSC - Command and General Staff Course	A course required by the Army for all officers to advance to the level of Lieutenant Colonel, the course was administered by the Command and General Staff College at Fort Leavenworth, Kansas. Today, the course is called ILE or Intermediate Level Education.
CA - Civil Affairs	Once known as Military Government units during World War II, it is a branch within the U.S. Army and Marine Corps. Civil Affairs units help military commanders by working with civil authorities and civilian populations in the commander's area of operations to lessen the impact of military operations on them during peace and combat operations. Most CA units are in the reserve, made up of citizen soldiers with rich skill sets including medical, veterinary, legal, education, civil engineering, arts and monuments, banking, labor relations, utility operations and more.
CIA - Central Intelligence Agency	U.S. Government agency responsible for providing national security intelligence to senior U.S. policymakers. The agency also oversees covert and direct action to destroy facilities and persons deemed threats to the security of the U.S..

CID - Criminal Investigation Division	A law enforcement branch of the Army and Navy, made up of special agents equivalent to detectives in a police force.
CJ2	Abbreviation for the Command's Intelligence Officer and staff.
COIN - Counter-Insurgency	A doctrine that calls for the protection of population centers while enhancing the legitimacy of the host nation government to enable the host nation government to win the loyalty of the population centers as opposed to the groups of insurgents.
COMISAF - Commander of ISAF	A four-star position held by a U.S. Officer.
CONEX	A shipping container that resembles the rectangular shaped back of a tractor-trailer. They are stacked, wired and furbished to act as offices and living quarters.
CONUS - Continental Unites States	The 48 contiguous states in the United States (that is, all the states except Alaska and Hawaii).
CRC - CONUS Replacement Center	Located at Fort Benning, Georgia, this is where soldiers deploying to a combat zone as an individual replacement instead of as part of a whole unit, go to get equipped, screened and trained for their deployment.
DFAC - Dining Facility	Dining Facility run by the military or a contractor for the military.

DoS - Department of State - State Department	The diplomatic agency of the United States that headed by the Secretary of State and answers to the President.
FORCEPRO - Force Protection	Units of soldiers trained to be respond to attacks on convoys or bases.
GI - General Issue	Equipment issued by the Army to all soldiers. It has become a slang term for a soldier. Also GI Joe.
GIROA - Government of the Islamic Republic of Afghanistan	The official term for the Afghan national government.
Green Zone	An area of high security where the Coalition has its embassies and headquarters elements located. In Afghanistan it is where the U.S. Embassy, ISAF Headquarters, Afghan Ministry of Defense, Afghan Presidential Palace and NATO Training Mission headquarters are located.
GS - General Staff	The senior leadership of the Afghan National Army broken down into staff functions, such as Personnel, Intelligence, Operations, Logistics, Information, Legal, Medical and more.
ID	Identification
IED - Improvised Explosive Device	The biggest killer of forces in Afghanistan, they are devices made of artillery shells or other explosive material and include detonators made from alarm clocks, garage door openers, cell phones or human pressed buttons. IEDs are buried in the road, placed in vehicles, donkey carts or suicide vests.

IG - Inspector General	A branch of officers that take complaints and investigate allegations that the military unit or individuals are not following their own rules, regulations and procedures. The Department of Defense and each branch of service have IG officers.
IJC - ISAF Joint Command	The IJC is in charge of all NATO combat forces in Afghanistan and is commanded by a U.S. three-star officer.
ILON - Inherent Law for Officers and Non Commission Officers	An Afghan personnel law for the Afghan military.
ISAF - International Security Assistance Force	This is the name of the NATO command in Afghanistan. A four-star U.S. officer is the commander of ISAF.
ISI - Inter-Services Intelligence	Pakistan's CIA.
JAG - Judge Advocate General	A term used for military lawyers who serve in uniform. It also refers to the most senior military lawyer who is a three-star officer - Army JAG, Air Force JAG and Navy JAG.
K9	A term used for military dogs and their handlers.
Kandak	A Kandak is an Afghan unit that is about the size of a U.S. battalion. A U.S. battalion is about three to five hundred soldiers. Kandaks and battalions are commanded by Lieutenant Colonels (O5).
MoD - Ministry of Defense	The Afghan Ministry of Defense, it controls the Afghan Army and Air Forces.

MoI - Ministry of Interior	The Afghan Ministry of Interior, it controls the police forces of Afghanistan
MRAP - Mine Resistant Ambush Protected Vehicle	Armored vehicles designed to better withstand IEDs planted in the roadways.
MTAG - Medical Training Advisory Group	A team of Coalition medical officers responsible for training the Afghan Security Force medical personnel.
MWR - Morale Welfare and Recreation	Activities designed to provide some comfort and morale boosting to the troops and their families. They include areas to smoke and drink coffee, computer banks for troops to access Facebook, Skype and email, and areas to read books and watch movies.

NATO/ OTAN - North Atlantic Treaty Organization/ Organisation du Traite de l'Atlantique Nord	A collection of countries that came together by treaty in 1949 in response to the threat of the Soviet Union against European Nations. The treaty declares in Article 5 that an attack on any member nation is an attack on all member nations. When Al Qaeda, led by Osama Bin Laden in Afghanistan, attacked the United States on September 11, 2001, the United States asked NATO to invoke Article 5, which is why NATO is operating in Afghanistan today. NATO continues to exist despite the breakup of the Soviet Union and its Warsaw Pact that was an alliance of communist nations. The Warsaw Pact nations, such as Poland and Slovakia were considered nations held against their people's will behind the Soviet's "Iron Curtain," a term coined by Winston Churchill. Many former Warsaw Pact nations are now members of NATO. NATO's most recent operation was in Libya to overthrow Qaddafi. The operation involved neither European territory nor an attack on a member nation.
NCO - Non Commissioned Officer	An enlisted soldier who reaches the rank of Corporal or higher. An NCO is like a foreman, someone who makes sure that the officers' plans and orders are carried out by the troops.
NDS - National Directorate for Security	The Afghan intelligence service.

NGOs - Non Governmental Organizations	Organizations that operates independently from any government. Examples include the International Committee for the Red Cross, Doctors without Borders, OXFAM, and Amnesty International to name a few.
NMH - National Military Hospital	Located in Kabul, the Afghans consider it the crown jewel of its medical capability.
Northern Alliance	A group of tribes, mostly Tajik, Uzbek and Hazara in northern Afghanistan that came together to resist the Taliban, which was made up of Pashtuns.
NPR - National Public Radio	A non-profit radio network in the U.S..
NTM-A - NATO Training Mission - Afghanistan	Created in November 2009 and headed by a three-star U.S. General, this command is responsible for recruiting, equipping and training Afghan Security Forces that include the Afghan National Army and the Afghan National Police. The NMT-A commander is also the commander of CSTC-A, the Combined Security Transition Command - Afghanistan. Today, CSTC-A is nothing more than a U.S. command on paper that provides U.S. Taxpayer funding for the Afghan Security Forces at the rate of one billion dollars a month.
OCT - Out of Country Training	A term referring to training Afghan soldiers and police obtain in countries other than Afghanistan.
OPSEC - Operational Security	Taking steps to protect information that the enemy would find useful to stop or interfere with U.S. Military operations.

PX - Post Exchange	A general store run by the Army and Air Force Exchange Service which sells merchandise to soldiers and their families on military bases at home and abroad, including in combat zones.
R&R - Rest and Relaxation	When soldiers are deployed to an area where combat is prevalent, also called a hostile fire zone or imminent danger zone, the government provides them with 15 days off to spend anywhere in the world. Most troops fly home for these 15 days, while others meet their families at a resort such as the Hotel Edelweiss in Garmish, Germany which is run by the Department of Defense.
REFORGER - Return of Forces to Germany	A cold war era exercise called Return of Forces to Germany. The exercise involved moving U.S. Armed forces from the U.S. to Germany as would be needed to stop an attack by the Soviet Union on western Europe. The exercise was designed to show the Soviets, and the U.S., that the U.S. could do so.
SAO - Security Assistance Office	Oversees training of Afghan forces in the U.S. and programs to deliver weapons and other supplies to Afghan Security Forces.

SF - Special Forces	Commonly known as Green Berets because of a song in 1967 and the Green Beret President Kennedy authorized them to wear when not in the field, these soldiers are highly trained, multi skilled professionals, many with advanced degrees and multi-language capable. To become a "tabbed" (a patch that reads "Special Forces" to wear on your left shoulder) SF soldier, one must complete a one year Q Course (qualification course) compared to the six week course for Army Rangers. All SF Soldiers are airborne qualified, meaning they are trained to jump out of an aircraft with a full load of combat equipment. SF Soldiers perform a variety of missions, including training of foreign military, direct action against high value targets and intelligence gathering. Special Forces soldiers wear a tab on their left shoulder that reads "SPECIAL FORCES." They are sometimes referred to as "Tabbed SF."
SIGAR - Special Inspector General for Afghan Reconstruction	Congress created the Office of the Special Inspector General for Afghanistan Reconstruction to provide independent and objective oversight of the 62 billion dollars in humanitarian and reconstruction assistance given to Afghanistan since 2002. http://www.sigar.mil/Objective_oversight.asp
Staff Judge Advocate	A military lawyer that functions as a general counsel to the local commander of a division or corps size unit.

Sunni and Shia Muslim	Sunni Muslims make up 85% of the Muslim world. Most Shia Muslims are located in Iran and Iraq. In the Islamic Republic of Afghanistan, most Afghans are Sunni. The minority Hazara Tribe are mostly Shia. The division between Shia and Sunni dates back to the death of the Prophet Muhammad, and the question of who was to take over the leadership of the Muslim nation. Sunni Muslims agree with the position taken by many of the Prophet's companions, that the new leader should be elected from among those capable of the job. This is what was done, and the Prophet Muhammad's close friend and advisor, Abu Bakr, became the first Caliph of the Islamic nation. The word "Sunni" in Arabic comes from a word meaning "one who follows the traditions of the Prophet." The Shia Muslims believe that following the Prophet Muhammad's death, leadership should have passed directly to his cousin/son-in-law, Ali. Throughout history, Shia Muslims have not recognized the authority of elected Muslim leaders, choosing instead to follow a line of Imams that they believe were appointed by the Prophet Muhammad or God Himself. The word "Shia" in Arabic means a group or supportive party of people.

USMA - United States Military Academy	The USMA is located at West Point, New York. It is a college that produces newly commissioned Second Lieutenants into the U.S. Army. Famous graduates include Presidents Dwight D. Eisenhower and Ulysses S Grant and Generals Robert E Lee, George Patton, Omar Bradley, Douglass MacArthur, Norman Schwarzkopf and David Petraeus.
USO - United Service Organizations	Millions of times each year at hundreds of locations around the world, the USO lifts the spirits of America's troops and their families. A nonprofit, congressionally chartered, private organization, the USO relies on the generosity of individuals, organizations and corporations to support its activities. The USO is not part of the U.S. government, but is recognized by the Department of Defense, Congress and President of the United States, who serves as Honorary Chairman of the USO.